3RD **Edition**

OREGON

YOUR CAR-CAMPING GUIDE TO SCENIC BEAUTY, THE SOUNDS
OF NATURE, AND AN ESCAPE FROM CIVILIZATION

Library of Congress Cataloging-in-Publication Data
Names: Ohlsen, Becky author.
Title: Best tent camping. Oregon : your car-camping guide to scenic beauty, the sounds of nature, and an escape
  from civilization / Becky Ohlsen.
Other titles: Best in tent camping, Oregon
Description: Third Edition. | Birmingham, Alabama : Menasha Ridge Press, An imprint of AdventureKEEN, [2018]
  | Previous edition: 2009, written by Jeanne Pyle and revised by Paul Gerald. | "Distributed by Publishers
  Group West"—T.p. verso. | Includes index.
Identifiers: LCCN 2018007306 | ISBN 9780897326773 (paperback) | ISBN 9780897326780 (ebook)
Subjects: LCSH: Camping—Oregon—Guidebooks. | Camp sites, facilities, etc.—Oregon—Guidebooks. | Outdoor
  recreation—Oregon—Guidebooks. | Oregon—Guidebooks.
Classification: LCC GV191.42.O7 P95 2018 | DDC 796.5409795—dc23
LC record available at https://lccn.loc.gov/2018007306

Cover and book design: Jonathan Norberg
Maps: Scott McGrew
Interior photos by Becky Ohlsen, except as noted on page and the following: page 35: Gail Johnson/Shutterstock; page
45: Ethan Quin/Shutterstock; page 63: HDDA Photography/Shutterstock; page 64: Catherine Avilez/Shutterstock; page
73: Ray Whittemore/Shutterstock; page 76: Kathleen Herman/Shutterstock; page 88: Bob Pool/Shutterstock; page 91:
Hills Outdoors/Shutterstock; page 94: Cory Seamer/Shutterstock
Cover photo: Elk Lake Campground (see page 48) by Becky Ohlsen; inset: Nestucca River National Back Country
Byway (see page 18) courtesy of Bureau of Land Management Oregon and Washington/Flickr/CC BY 2.0
(creativecommons.org/licenses/by/2.0)

 MENASHA RIDGE PRESS
An imprint of AdventureKEEN
2204 First Ave. S, Ste. 102
Birmingham, AL 35233
800-443-7227, fax 205-326-1012

Visit menasharidge.com for a complete listing of our books and for ordering information. Contact us at our website, at
facebook.com/menasharidge, or at twitter.com/menasharidge with questions or comments. To find out more about
who we are and what we're doing, visit blog.menasharidge.com.

3RD Edition

BEST TENT Camping

OREGON

YOUR CAR-CAMPING GUIDE TO SCENIC BEAUTY, THE SOUNDS OF NATURE, AND AN ESCAPE FROM CIVILIZATION

Becky Ohlsen

MENASHA RIDGE PRESS
Your Guide to the Outdoors Since 1982

Oregon Campground Locator Map

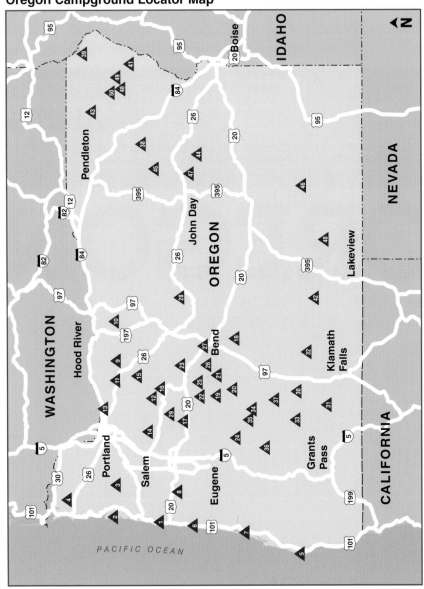

CONTENTS

Map Legend

Paved roads	Unpaved roads	Trails	Water features	Forest/park

Camping icons

- 🏠 Cabins
- ⛺ Campground
- Equestrian campsite
- Group campsite (general)
- Group campsite (numbered)
- Group shelter
- Hiker/biker campsite
- Host tent site
- Tent site (general)
- Tent site (numbered)

Other icons

- Amphitheater
- Beach access
- Biking trail
- Boat launch
- Bridge
- Campfire
- Camping restricted
- Corral
- Dam
- Drinking water
- Dump station
- Fee station
- Firewood
- Fish-cleaning station
- Gate
- General point of interest
- Hiking trail
- Horseshoe pit
- Information
- Laundry

- Marina
- Mine/quarry
- Overlook
- Parking
- Park office
- Phone access
- Picnic area
- Picnic (group area)
- Picnic shelter
- Playground
- Recycling bins
- Restrooms
- Restrooms (primitive)
- Showers
- Spring
- Store
- Swimming access
- Scenic view
- Trash bins
- Wheelchair access

ACKNOWLEDGMENTS

Thanks to all the friends, family, and random strangers who, to my surprise, were happy to share a secret or two when I asked them about their favorite campgrounds in Oregon. (Of course, there's no rule against keeping a *few* places to yourself; discovering your own favorites is half the fun!) Also, thanks to Paul Gerald for putting together a solid second edition for me to revise, and to the folks at AdventureKEEN for asking me to do it. Thanks to my grandparents Dorothy and Bob Ohlsen for lending me the van that became my mobile office, and to my expert copilot, a great traveler, stargazer, snack maker, map reader, and card shark. Finally, huge thanks to everyone at the U.S. Forest Service, the Bureau of Land Management, and all the park staff and volunteers who keep these campgrounds in tip-top shape and who provided helpful updates, advice, campground layouts, and other vital information to make these entries as accurate as possible.

—Becky Ohlsen

Welcome to Paradise: Camping in Oregon means everything from alpine lakes and high deserts to lush riverside hideaways, such as Paradise Campground in the Central Cascades (see page 79).

PREFACE

Looking back, most of us can probably summon up a formative tent-camping experience—something that defined for us early on what it means to go camping. Mine involved rain. A lot of rain. I was about 10 years old, and my dad had decided to take my brother and me away for a weekend camping trip in the woods. Mom stayed behind for some much-anticipated peace and quiet. The trip did not go quite as planned. Turns out, when you come back to camp at the end of a long cold day of fishing and hiking to find that the miserable downpour has left you, your camping gear, and both of your children thoroughly, irreparably drenched, the only sound decision is to pack everybody back into the van and drive home. (Needless to say, this was not quite the way my mom had hoped the trip would go either. She had just settled in with a cup of tea and a good book when our soggy crew trudged in two days ahead of schedule, dripping, whining, and offering up our wet sleeping bags for her to deal with.)

In retrospect, it was lucky I went on that trip, however abbreviated it was. The early association between camping and rain prepared me well for years of pitching tents in Oregon, where, even in mid-July, it's seldom a good idea to leave off the rainfly.

Like it or not, rain is a defining characteristic of camping across Oregon for much of the year. Mind you, it's not as bad as people say: August is pretty reliably warm and dry. Of course, that brings the threat of wildfires, which seem to tear through different parts of the state every year. It's all part of the cycle, and camping here means resigning yourself to whatever diabolical—or, if you're lucky, delightful—plans nature has in mind.

But in exchange for a bit of dramatic weather, Oregon gets velvety glacial valleys, thick old-growth forests, glimmering lakes, thunderous waterfalls, roaring rivers, snowcapped peaks, stunning hillsides full of spring wildflowers, lush rainforests where moss-draped trees shake hands across creekbeds, magical deserts, a vivid green coastline, and just about everything in between—not to mention all the wild creatures that live in each of these habitats.

As anyone who's spent any time traveling here knows, Oregon is a place of unparalleled beauty and diversity. Extremes of climate, terrain, and vegetation can be experienced in a single day's outing. In a few hours, you can drive from the Blue Mountains to Hells Canyon and feel like you've gone interstellar. The southeast corner of the state could not be more different from the southwest: arid, expansive, and dotted with mustangs on the one hand; lush, green, and stormy on the other. The campgrounds included in this book offer a sample of the variety that makes Oregon such a prized destination for those who seek outstanding outdoor adventures. But keep in mind that it's only a sample; there are plenty of unexplored corners of the state, hidden places that might be right around the corner from some of the places we describe here. As you use this book, be sure to supplement it with your own sense of adventure and discovery. As for things to do once you reach your chosen campground, we provide some leads here, but there's bound to be more than we can pack into one book. Explore as much as you have time for—you won't regret it.

If you're the sort who values solitude and serenity above all else, you may have to seek adventure farther afield than most other people. (That is, unless you're up for some backcountry camping—there are loads of great backpacking options within an easy drive of Portland.) Oregonians and our neighbors are active users of the great outdoors; car camping is popular here, and the best-known sites are bound to be crowded, especially in summer. (Blame the rain, if you like.) To escape the crowds, you'll need to drive farther, climb higher, and plan more creatively—or be more spontaneous. Why not see what's at the end of that mysterious dirt road? Be aware that it takes a good chunk of time to reach some of the more interesting and far-flung corners of the state, but it's well worth the effort. Our advice: Load up the car, settle in for a long drive, and enjoy the journey as much as the destination.

REGIONS IN THIS BOOK

Oregon contains an astounding variety of terrain, from rainforest to high desert and just about everything in between. Probably the most obvious distinction is the one separating the western and eastern parts of the state, in climate, terrain, and even lifestyle. The rugged coast and the Cascade Mountains, which run north–south through the state, are generally considered western Oregon, while eastern Oregon (larger and sparsely populated) includes vast stretches of arid land. For ease in planning your trip, we have further grouped campgrounds into six regions, dividing those along the coast into northern and southern groups; dividing those in the Cascades into northern, central, and southern groups; and presenting the scattered offerings of eastern Oregon in a single group.

The North Fork of the Malheur River provides a scenic backdrop to its eponymous campground (see page 147).

photographed by Musgrove and the Pumi

BEST
CAMPGROUNDS

BEST FOR EQUESTRIANS

BEST FOR FAMILIES WITH KIDS

BEST FOR FISHING AND BOATING

BEST FOR SWIMMING

Yellowbottom Campground (see page 100) sits near rocky Quartzville Creek.

INTRODUCTION

HOW TO USE THIS GUIDEBOOK

The publishers of Menasha Ridge Press welcome you to *Best Tent Camping: Oregon*. Whether you are new to this activity or have been sleeping in your portable outdoor shelter over decades of outdoor adventures, please review the following information. It explains how we have worked with the author to organize this book and how you can make the best use of it.

THE RATINGS & RATING CATEGORIES

This guidebook's author personally experienced dozens of campgrounds and campsites to select the top 50 locations in this state. Within that universe of 50 sites, the author then ranked each one in the six categories described below. As a tough grader, the author awarded few five-star ratings, but each campground in this guidebook is superlative in its own way. For example, a site may be rated only one star in one category but perhaps five stars in another category. This rating system allows you to choose your destination based on the attributes that are most important to you:

★★★★★   The site is **ideal** in that category.

★★★★   The site is **exemplary** in that category.

★★★   The site is **very good** in that category.

★★   The site is **above average** in that category.

★   The site is **acceptable** in that category.

BEAUTY

Beauty, of course, is in the eye of the beholder, but panoramic views or proximity to a lake or river earn especially high marks. A campground that blends in well with the environment scores well, as do areas with remarkable wildlife or geology. Well-kept vegetation and nicely laid-out sites also up the ratings.

PRIVACY

The number of sites in a campground, the amount of screening between them, and physical distance from one another are decisive factors for the privacy ratings. Other considerations include the presence of nearby trails or day-use areas, and proximity to a town or city that would invite regular day-use traffic and perhaps compromise privacy.

SPACIOUSNESS

The size of the tent spot, its proximity to other tent spots, and whether or not it is defined or bordered from activity areas are the key consideration. The highest ratings go to sites that allow the tent camper to comfortably spread out without overlapping neighboring sites or picnic, cooking, or parking areas.

QUIET

Criteria for this rating include several touchstones: the author's experience at the site, the nearness of roads, the proximity of towns and cities, the probable number of RVs, the likelihood of noisy all-terrain vehicles or boats, and whether a campground host is available or willing to enforce the quiet hours. Of course, one set of noisy neighbors can deflate a five-star rating into a one-star (or no-star), so the latter criterion—campground enforcement—was particularly important in the author's evaluation in this category.

SECURITY

How you determine a campground's security will depend on who you view as the greater risk: other people or the wilderness. The more remote the campground, the less likely you are to run into opportunistic crime but the harder it is to get help in case of an accident or dangerous wildlife confrontation. Ratings in this category take into consideration whether there is a campground host or resident park ranger, proximity of other campers' sites, how much day traffic the campground receives, how close the campground is to a town or city, and whether there is cell phone reception or some type of phone or emergency call button.

CLEANLINESS

A campground's appearance often depends on who was there right before you and how your visit coincides with the maintenance schedule. In general, higher marks went to those campgrounds with hosts who cleaned up regularly. The rare case of odor-free toilets also gleaned high marks. At unhosted campgrounds, criteria included trash receptacles and evidence that sites were cleared and that signs and buildings were kept repaired. Markdowns for the campground were not given for a single visitor's garbage left at a site, but old trash in the shrubbery and along trails, indicating infrequent cleaning, did secure low ratings.

THE CAMPGROUND LOCATOR MAP & MAP LEGEND

Use the campground locator map on page iv to pinpoint the location of each campground. Each campground's number follows it throughout this guidebook: from that campground locator map, to the table of contents, and to the profile's first page. A map legend that details the symbols found on the campground-layout maps appears on page vii.

CAMPGROUND-LAYOUT MAPS

Each profile contains a detailed map of campground sites, internal roads, facilities, and other key items.

CAMPGROUND ENTRANCE GPS COORDINATES

All of the profiles in this guidebook include the GPS coordinates for each site entrance. The intersection of the latitude (north) and longitude (west) coordinates orient you at the entrance. Please note that this guidebook uses the degree–decimal minute format for presenting the GPS coordinates. Example:

N44° 43.715' W124° 03.345'

To convert GPS coordinates from degrees, minutes, and seconds to the above degree–decimal minute format, the seconds are divided by 60. For more on GPS technology, visit usgs.gov.

WEATHER

Prevailing conditions year-round (with a few exceptions) in western Oregon are mild and damp: not so much rain as a healthy supply of gray clouds and mist. Areas like the Willamette Valley on the eastern flanks of the Coast Range can get quite hot and steamy, but a short drive up and over the range to the coastal areas and you'll be reaching for the fleece as the inversion effect creates fog banks and cool breezes. Late summer and early fall are the most dependable seasons for lovely stints of dry, sunny, warm days just about anywhere in western Oregon.

In eastern Oregon, conditions are desert-like, with hot and dry summers. Severe thunderstorms can be the biggest threat to outdoor activity and, in turn, can spark wildfires and flash floods. At higher elevations on both western and eastern mountain slopes, snow is common, even in midsummer. Sudden changes in weather conditions are always a consideration, so pack accordingly.

FIRST AID KIT

A useful first aid kit may contain more items than you might think necessary. These are just the basics. Prepackaged kits in waterproof bags are available. As a preventive measure, always take along sunscreen and insect repellent. Even though quite a few items are listed here, they pack down into a small space:

- Adhesive bandages, such as Band-Aids

- Antibiotic ointment (Neosporin or the generic equivalent)

- Antiseptic or disinfectant, such as Betadine or hydrogen peroxide

- Benadryl or the generic equivalent, diphenhydramine (in case of allergic reactions)

- Butterfly-closure bandages

- Elastic bandages or joint wraps

- Emergency poncho

- Epinephrine in a prefilled syringe (for severe allergic reactions to bee stings, etc.)

- Gauze (one roll and six 4-by-4-inch pads)

- Ibuprofen or acetaminophen

- Insect repellent

- LED flashlight or headlamp

- Matches or pocket lighter

- Mirror for signaling passing aircraft

- Moleskin/Spenco 2nd Skin

- Pocketknife or multipurpose tool

- Sunscreen/lip balm

- Waterproof first aid tape

- Whistle (it's more effective in signaling rescuers than your voice)

FLORA & FAUNA PRECAUTIONS

POISONOUS PLANTS

Recognizing poison ivy, oak, and sumac and avoiding contact with them are the most effective ways to prevent the painful, itchy rashes associated with these plants. Poison ivy ranges from a thick, tree-hugging vine to a shaded ground cover, 3 leaflets to a leaf; poison oak occurs as either a vine or shrub, with 3 leaflets as well; and poison sumac flourishes in swampland, each leaf containing 7–13 leaflets. Urushiol, the oil in the sap of these plants, is responsible for the rash. Usually within 12–14 hours of exposure (but sometimes much later), raised lines and/or blisters will appear, accompanied by a terrible itch. Refrain from scratching because bacteria under fingernails can cause infection. Wash and dry the rash thoroughly, applying a calamine lotion or other product to help dry out the rash. If itching or blistering is severe, seek medical attention. Remember that oil-contaminated clothes, pets, or hiking gear can easily cause an irritating rash on you or someone else, so wash not only any exposed parts of your body but also clothes, gear, and pets.

Poison oak

photographed by Jane Huber

MOSQUITOES

Mosquitoes are common in Oregon, especially from spring through mid-summer. Though it's very rare, individuals can become infected with the West Nile virus by being bitten by an infected mosquito. Culex mosquitoes, the primary varieties that can transmit West Nile virus to humans, thrive in urban rather than natural areas. They lay their eggs in stagnant water and can breed in any standing water that remains for more than five days. Most people infected with West Nile virus have no symptoms of illness, but some may become ill, usually 3–15 days after being bitten.

Anytime you expect mosquitoes to be buzzing around, you may want to wear protective clothing, such as long sleeves, long pants, and socks. Loose-fitting, light-colored clothing is best. Spray clothing with insect repellent. Remember to follow the instructions on the repellent and to take extra care to protect children against these insects.

SNAKES

Rattlesnakes, corals, copperheads, and cottonmouths are among the most common venomous snakes in the United States, and hibernation season is typically October–April.

In some of the regions described in this book, you may encounter rattlesnakes. They like to bask in the sun and won't bite unless threatened. Most of the snakes you will see while hiking, however, will be nonvenomous species and subspecies. The best rule is to leave all snakes alone, give them a wide berth as you hike past, and make sure any hiking companions (including dogs) do the same.

When hiking, stick to well-used trails, and wear over-the-ankle boots and loose-fitting long pants. Do not step or put your hands

Rattlesnake

photographed by Jane Huber

beyond your range of detailed visibility, and avoid wandering around in the dark. Step onto logs and rocks, never over them, and be especially careful when climbing rocks. Always avoid walking through dense brush or willow thickets.

TICKS

Ticks are often found on brush and tall grass, where they seem to be waiting to hitch a ride on a warm-blooded passerby. Adult ticks are most active April–May and again October–November. Among the varieties of ticks, the black-legged tick, commonly called the deer tick, is the primary carrier of Lyme disease, but documented cases of Lyme in Oregon are extremely rare. Ticks here are more a nuisance than a serious health risk (although tick bites always carry the risk of infection, so properly disinfecting the area is key). Wear light-colored clothing to make it easier for you to spot ticks before they migrate to your skin. At the end of the hike, visually check your hair, back of neck, armpits, and socks. During your posthike shower, take a moment to do a more complete body check. For ticks that are already embedded, removal with tweezers is best. Grasp the tick close to your skin, and remove it by pulling straight out firmly. Do your best to remove the head, but do not twist. Use disinfectant solution on the wound.

ROADS & VEHICLES

Many of the campgrounds in this book are reached by minimally maintained access roads. Additionally, some access roads are closed during winter, opening only once the snow is cleared. Always inquire about current road conditions before venturing too far, especially early or late in the season or if there have been recent wildfires in the area.

Be sure that you have a current road atlas with you. The maps in this book are designed to help orient you, nothing more. Although we've provided directions at the end of each entry, you'll still need a proper map of the area. The local and district offices that oversee most of these campgrounds are the best source for detailed maps (see Appendix B for more information on these agencies).

RESTRICTIONS & PERMITS

State and federal agencies manage most of the campgrounds in this book. Check with the proper authorities for current regulations on recreational activities, such as permits for day-use parking, backcountry travel, hunting and fishing, mountain bikes in designated areas, and so on. Many day-use areas in Oregon require a fee; these are often covered by the annual Northwest Forest Pass, available online (store.usgs.gov/forest-pass), at ranger stations, or from many outdoor retailers. We have included some restrictions in the Key Information sections of each campground description, but because restrictions can change, you still need to check before you go.

FIRES

Campfire regulations are subject to seasonal conditions. Usually signs are posted at campgrounds or ranger district offices. Please be aware of the current situation and NEVER make a campfire anywhere other than in existing fire rings at developed sites. Never, ever toss a match or cigarette idly in the brush or alongside the road. It's not only littering, but it can also trigger the incineration of that beautiful forest you were just admiring.

WATER

Many of the campgrounds in this book are remote enough that piped water is not available. No matter how remote you may think you are, though, don't risk drinking straight from mountain streams, creeks, and lakes. Oregon has some of the purest natural waters in the world, but it is not immune to that nasty parasite called *Giardia lamblia*, which causes horrific stomach cramps and long-term diarrhea. If you don't have drinking water or purification tablets with you, boil any untreated water for a full minute, or at least three minutes in high altitude.

CAMPGROUND ETIQUETTE

Here are a few tips on how to create good vibes with fellow campers and wildlife you encounter.

- **MAKE SURE YOU CHECK IN, PAY YOUR FEE, AND MARK YOUR SITE AS DIRECTED.** Don't make the mistake of grabbing a seemingly empty site that looks more appealing than your site. It could be reserved. If you're unhappy with the site you've selected, check with the campground host for other options.

- **BE SENSITIVE TO THE GROUND BENEATH YOU.** Be sure to place all garbage in designated receptacles or pack it out if none are available. No one likes to see the trash someone else has left behind.

- **IT'S COMMON FOR ANIMALS TO WANDER THROUGH CAMPSITES,** where they may be accustomed to the presence of humans (and our food). An unannounced approach, a sudden movement, or a loud noise startles most animals. A surprised animal can be dangerous to you, to others, and to themselves. Give them plenty of space. Use bear-proof food boxes when they are available.

- **PLAN AHEAD.** Know your equipment, your ability, and the area where you are camping—and prepare accordingly. Be self-sufficient at all times; carry necessary supplies for changes in weather or other conditions. A well-executed trip is a satisfaction to you and to others.

- **BE COURTEOUS TO OTHER CAMPERS,** hikers, bikers, and anyone else you encounter.

- **STRICTLY FOLLOW THE CAMPGROUND'S RULES REGARDING THE BUILDING OF FIRES**—and keep in mind that these may change depending on seasonal fire risk levels. Never burn trash. Trash smoke smells horrible, and trash debris in a fire ring or grill is unsightly.

HAPPY CAMPING

With a little planning, it's easy to have a great camping trip. To assist with making your outing a happy one, here are some pointers:

- **RESERVE YOUR SITE IN ADVANCE,** especially if it's a weekend or a holiday, or if the campground is wildly popular. Many prime campgrounds require at least a six-month lead time on reservations. Check before you go.

- **PICK YOUR CAMPING BUDDIES WISELY.** A family trip is pretty straightforward, but you may want to reconsider including grumpy Uncle Fred, who doesn't like bugs, sunshine, or marshmallows. After you know who's going, make sure that everyone is on the same page regarding expectations of difficulty (amenities or the lack thereof, physical exertion, and so on), sleeping arrangements, and food requirements.

- **DON'T DUPLICATE EQUIPMENT,** such as cooking pots and lanterns, among campers in your party. Carry what you need to have a good time, but don't turn the trip into a cross-country moving experience.

- **DRESS FOR THE SEASON.** Educate yourself on the temperature highs and lows of the specific part of the state you plan to visit. It may be warm at night in the summer in your backyard, but up in the mountains it can be quite chilly. In the shoulder season, be sure to check road conditions and forecasts before you set out.

- **PITCH YOUR TENT ON A LEVEL SURFACE,** preferably one covered with leaves, pine straw, or grass. Use a tarp or specially designed footprint to thwart ground moisture and to protect the tent floor. Do a little site maintenance, such as picking up the small rocks and sticks that can damage your tent floor and make sleep uncomfortable. If you have a separate tent rainfly but don't think you'll need it, keep it rolled up at the base of the tent in case it starts raining at midnight.

- **CONSIDER TAKING A SLEEPING PAD** if the ground makes you uncomfortable. Choose a pad that is full-length and thicker than you think you might need. This will not only keep your hips from aching on hard ground but will also help keep you warm. A wide range of thin, light, and inflatable pads is available at camping stores, and these are a much better choice than home air mattresses, which conduct heat away from the body and tend to deflate during the night.

- **IF YOU ARE NOT HIKING IN TO A PRIMITIVE CAMPSITE, THERE IS NO REAL NEED TO SKIMP ON FOOD DUE TO WEIGHT.** Plan tasty meals and bring everything you will need to prepare, cook, eat, and clean up. And don't forget to bring plenty of your beverage of choice, and more water than you think you'll need.

- **IF YOU TEND TO USE THE BATHROOM MULTIPLE TIMES AT NIGHT, YOU SHOULD PLAN AHEAD.** Leaving a warm sleeping bag and stumbling around in the dark to find the restroom, whether it be a pit toilet, a fully plumbed comfort station, or just the woods, is not fun. Keep a flashlight or headlamp and any other accoutrements you may need by the tent door, and know exactly where to head in the dark.

- **STANDING DEAD TREES AND STORM-DAMAGED LIVING TREES CAN POSE A REAL HAZARD TO TENT CAMPERS.** These trees may have loose or broken limbs that could fall at any time. When choosing a campsite or even just a spot to rest during a hike, look up.

A WORD ABOUT BACKCOUNTRY CAMPING

Following these guidelines will increase your chances for a pleasant, safe, and low-impact experience with nature.

Adhere to the adages "Pack it in, pack it out" and "Take only pictures, leave only footprints." Practice Leave No Trace camping ethics (lnt.org) while in the backcountry.

Every year in Oregon, wildfires cause significant damage, and regional fire bans are common. Before you consider lighting a campfire, check to make sure the forest service hasn't issued a ban. Never light campfires in the backcountry. Backpacking stoves are strongly encouraged.

Hang food away from bears and other animals to prevent them from becoming introduced to (and dependent on) human food. Wildlife quickly learns to associate backpacks and backpackers with easy food sources, thereby influencing their behavior.

Bury solid human waste in a hole at least 3 inches deep and at least 200 feet away from trails and water sources; a trowel is basic backpacking equipment. In some areas, the practice of burying human waste has been banned. Using a portable latrine (which comes in various incarnations, basically a glorified plastic bag, given out by park rangers) may seem unthinkable at first, but it's really no big deal. Just bring an extralarge zip-top bag for additional insurance against structural failures.

VENTURING AWAY FROM THE CAMPGROUND

If you go for a hike, bike ride, or other excursion into the wilderness—and you should!—here are some precautions to keep in mind:

- **ALWAYS CARRY FOOD AND WATER, WHETHER YOU ARE PLANNING TO GO OVERNIGHT OR NOT.** Food will give you energy, help keep you warm, and sustain you in an emergency until help arrives. Bring potable water, or treat water by boiling or filtering before drinking from a lake or stream.

- **STAY ON DESIGNATED TRAILS.** Most hikers who get lost do so because they leave the trail. Even on the most clearly marked trails, there is usually a point where you have to stop and consider which direction to head. If you become disoriented, don't panic. As soon as you think you may be off-track, stop, assess your current direction, and then retrace your steps back to the point where you went awry. If you have absolutely no idea how to continue, return to the trailhead the way you came in. Should you become completely lost and have no idea of how to return to the trailhead, remaining in place along the trail and waiting for help is most often the best option for adults and always the best option for children.

- **BE ESPECIALLY CAREFUL WHEN CROSSING STREAMS.** Whether you are fording the stream or crossing on a log, make every step count. If you have any doubt about maintaining your balance on a log, go ahead and ford the stream instead. When fording a stream, use a trekking pole or stout stick for balance and face upstream as you cross. If a stream seems too deep to ford, turn back. Whatever is on the other side is not worth risking your life.

- **BE CAREFUL AT OVERLOOKS.** Though these areas may provide spectacular views, they are potentially hazardous. Stay back from the edge of outcrops and be absolutely sure of your footing: a misstep can mean a nasty and possibly fatal fall.

- **KNOW THE SYMPTOMS OF HYPOTHERMIA.** Shivering and forgetfulness are the two most common indicators of this insidious killer. Hypothermia can occur at any elevation, even in the summer. Wearing cotton clothing puts you especially at risk, because cotton, when wet, draws heat away from the body. To prevent hypothermia, dress in layers using synthetic clothing for insulation, use a cap and gloves to reduce heat loss, and protect yourself with water-proof, breathable outerwear. If symptoms arise, get the victim to shelter, a fire, hot liquids, and dry clothes or a dry sleeping bag.

- **BRING YOUR BRAIN.** A cool, calculating mind is the single most important piece of equipment you'll ever need on the trail. Think before you act. Watch your step. Plan ahead. Avoiding accidents before they happen is the best recipe for a rewarding and relaxing hike.

CHANGES

While campgrounds are less prone to change than big-time tourist attractions, they are nevertheless subject to agency budgets, upgrades and dilapidation, and even natural disasters. With that in mind, it's a good idea to call ahead for the most updated report on the campground you've selected. We appreciate being told about any notable changes that you come across while using this book and welcome all reader input, including suggestions for potential entries for future editions. Send them to Menasha Ridge Press at the address provided on the copyright page, in care of Becky Ohlsen.

NORTHERN COAST

Beverly Beach (see page 12)

△ Beverly Beach State Park Campground

Beauty ★★★★ Privacy ★★★ Spaciousness ★★★★ Quiet ★★ Security ★★★ Cleanliness ★★★★

You can walk to the beach from your tent site through a tunnel under the highway, allowing for front-row seats to watch the sunset.

While you may think of the Pacific Coast as a summer destination, Oregon steps to the beat of a different drummer. Many people flock to the rugged Oregon coast to watch the winter storms and look out for whales. In fact, the prime whale watching months are late December–mid-March, when volunteers set up camp specifically to help you spot the spouts at prime locations along the coast. (If you're not sure where to start your whale watching efforts, head to the town of Depoe Bay, where Oregon State Parks runs the Depoe Bay Whale Watching Center, a facility devoted to giving visitors the best chance of spotting whales, as well as answering questions and sharing information.)

Located 7 miles north of Newport, Beverly Beach is a must-stay campground if you're in the area. While many of the surrounding campgrounds can get overloaded with RVs and consequently feel a little cramped, this campground manages to host everyone and still make you feel like you've gotten away from it all (and from your neighbor). The sites are spacious and wooded, and a nature trail winds its way through the campground, so you can start your day with a little exercise.

A nature trail winds its way through Beverly Beach State Park Campground.

KEY INFORMATION

CONTACT: 541-265-9278, 800-452-5687, oregonstateparks.org

OPEN: Year-round

SITES: 128 tent, 76 electric, 53 full hookup, 21 yurts, 3 group

WHEELCHAIR ACCESS: Restrooms; sites F10, F11, and F34; yurts A06, A08, A25, A26, F27, and F36

EACH SITE HAS: Picnic table, fire ring

ASSIGNMENT: First come, first served, or by reservation at 800-452-5687 or reserveamerica.com

REGISTRATION: At campground entrance

AMENITIES: Flush toilets, hot showers

PARKING: At campsites only; 1 vehicle/site; $7/additional vehicle

FEE: Tent $21, electric $31, full hookup $34, yurts $47; $8 reservation fee

ELEVATION: Sea level

RESTRICTIONS:

PETS: On leash only

QUIET HOURS: 10 p.m.–6 a.m.

FIRES: In fire rings only

ALCOHOL: Permitted

OTHER: 14-day stay limit

The most scenic part of the nature trail follows Spencer Creek, which borders the campground to the south. (Access the trail from the C Loop near site C3.) After crossing Spencer Creek, the trail splits. Walking to the right takes you to the hiker/biker camp. Head left to walk along the creek. The trail follows the creek to a bridge crossing located in the G Loop. Note that in spring and fall, the trail may be a bit of a muddy mess.

If you like to bicycle, park roads are open to bikes (helmets required). And in case you didn't bring your own wheels, you can rent a fat-tire bicycle from the Spencer Creek Welcome Center (at the campground entrance) for $20 a day.

Divided into eight loops, the campground is large, with 128 tent sites—trailers of any kind are wisely forbidden in the tent-camping areas. There are also three group tent-camping areas.

One attraction of this campground is that you can walk to the beach from your tent site through a tunnel under the highway, allowing for front-row seats to watch the sunset. While some sites are closer to the beach, they tend to get bombarded with visitors, so don't be fooled into thinking those are the best spots. Generally, the farther you are from the beach, the more likely you are to have some solitude. If you like to surf, the north beach is recommended. If you want to look for fossils, walk south along the beach.

With a general store nearby, firewood available at the campground, and a campground entrance station where staff will fill you in on the recreation hot spots—not to mention flush toilets and hot showers—Beverly Beach is a prime spot for tent-camping luxury with some elbow room.

Hiking is a popular activity here, with plenty of lighthouses (in particular, the Yaquina Head lighthouse is just south of the campground) and viewpoints to explore right off famous US 101. Of course, simply driving is a sightseeing adventure in itself, and the sweeping cliffside views of waves crashing below will tempt you to get out of your car and take advantage of the many viewpoints along US 101. Just north of Cape Foulweather, visit Depoe Bay and its remarkable spouting horn. When ocean waves surge into rocky tunnels along the shore, the spout erupts à la Old Faithful. Depoe Bay is also a great place to watch for whales.

In Newport, just south of Beverly Beach, you can get a fix of coastal city charm plus local seafood and microbrews along the historic waterfront. Established in 1882, Newport sits on the Yaquina Bay waterfront and has a few boat-charter companies, if you want to get out on the water; it's also home to the excellent Oregon Coast Aquarium.

In fact, there's so much to do in the surrounding area, it's a good thing Beverly Beach is open year-round, so you can pick your pleasure.

Beverly Beach State Park Campground

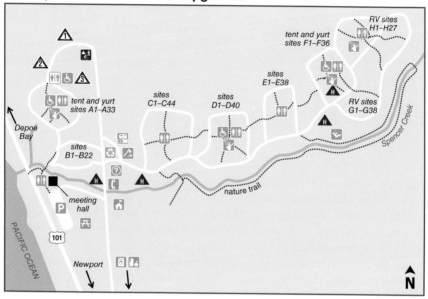

GETTING THERE

From I-5 take Exit 233 in Albany. Head west on US 20, and go 2 miles. Use the right lane to take the US 20 ramp to Corvallis, and go 10.8 miles to Corvallis. Turn right onto NW Harrison Boulevard, and drive just 0.1 mile; turn left onto NW Fourth Street and drive 0.7 mile. Then keep right to continue onto US 20 W and drive 48.2 miles to Newport. Turn right onto US 101 N and drive 6.3 miles. Turn right (east) into the park.

GPS COORDINATES: N44° 43.715'   W124° 03.345'

Cape Lookout State Park Campground

Beauty ★★★★★ Privacy ★★★★ Spaciousness ★★★ Quiet ★★★ *(summer)* ★★★★ *(winter)* Security ★★★★
Cleanliness ★★★★★

Despite the number of campsites, there is a spaciousness and openness about the place.

Just south of Netarts, the lovely and linear Cape Lookout State Park is one of three campgrounds on Three Capes Scenic Drive. The route actually encompasses two more state parks with (as you may have guessed from the road's name) magnificent headlands—Cape Meares on the north and Cape Kiwanda on the south—but these are day-use facilities only.

Capes Lookout, Meares, and Kiwanda are the centerpiece of more than 2,500 acres of coastal rain forest, sheer cliffs, wide sandy beaches and dunes, narrow spits, rocky points and outcrops, protected bays, and estuaries.

To accommodate the sizable numbers of seashore enthusiasts, the well-maintained and efficiently designed Cape Lookout State Park offers a whopping 173 tent sites, many of which are accessible all year. In addition, it offers a separate (and quieter) hiker/biker camp not far from the central camping grounds. Group camps are also available, as well as a meeting hall and four cabins. Despite the number of campsites, there is a spaciousness and openness about the place so that it feels—dare I say it?—uncrowded. That's not likely to be the case on any given summer day, but enjoy the feeling when you can. It's due in large part to the fact that when you have your back to the cape, the view is mainly of sand dunes, saltwater, and sky, a heady combination that encourages mindless meandering and musing.

Views of sea and sky are part of what makes Cape Lookout so alluring.

KEY INFORMATION

CONTACT: 503-842-4981, 800-551-6949, oregonstateparks.org

OPEN: Year-round

SITES: 173 tent, 38 full hookup, 1 electric, 13 yurts, 1 group, 6 cabins, 1 hiker/biker camp

WHEELCHAIR ACCESS: Restrooms, showers; sites C35 and C37; yurts 43, 44, 50, and 52

EACH SITE HAS: Picnic table, fire ring with grill, piped water

ASSIGNMENT: First come, first served, or by reservation at 800-452-5687 or reserveamerica.com

REGISTRATION: Self-registration on-site

AMENITIES: Flush toilets, hot water, showers; day-use area has picnic tables, grills, and beach access

PARKING: At campsites; $7/additional vehicle

FEE: Tent $21, electric $31, full hookup $34, yurts $47; $8 reservation fee

ELEVATION: Sea level

RESTRICTIONS:

PETS: On leash only

QUIET HOURS: 10 p.m.–6 a.m.

FIRES: In fire rings only

ALCOHOL: Permitted

OTHER: 14-day stay limit

For those of you who insist on a mission, consider shell collecting, bird-watching, or whale spotting (at the right times of year).

Geologically speaking, it may come as a surprise that the exquisite cape formations in this area and all along the Oregon Coast are the wind-, weather-, and wave-carved remains of ancient volcanoes. Geologists speculate that massive Cape Lookout, which many people consider one of the most scenic capes in the Northwest, was originally formed as an island off the coast when a huge lava flow cooled and congealed at different rates above and below sea level. You can observe the geologic layers from the base of this 700-foot promontory. The Cape Meares formation occurred similarly.

Cape Kiwanda, however, is essentially compressed sand made into rock and then shoved upward. Its sandstone composition would normally make Cape Kiwanda a fragile target of the pounding surf, but, as if by a master plan, nature provided the lofty point with its own Haystack Rock. (The more famous one is farther north, off the coast of Cannon Beach.) This giant piece of basalt encumbers incoming waves so effectively that fishing boats can head directly into the subdued breakers. In honor of this phenomenon, Pacific City (south of Cape Kiwanda) holds the Pacific City Dory Days festival each summer, showing off the seafaring talents of its famous fleet of flat-bottomed boats.

The Cape Meares cliffs are the nesting grounds for a wide variety of shorebirds that are protected, along with their forest-dwelling counterparts, by Cape Meares National Wildlife Refuge and Three Arch Rock National Wildlife Refuge in Oceanside. Between the two refuges, more than 150 species of birds are known to inhabit the shores and uplands. Cape Meares is also the site of the Octopus Tree, a Sitka spruce gone wild, with an inordinate number of drooping branches—well worth the short trek out to see and snap a photo. Historic Tillamook Rock Lighthouse on Cape Meares is the structural centerpiece of this park. You'll also have a decent chance of seeing elk on the Cape Meares Hiking Trail.

The average 90 inches of annual rainfall keep things fairly wet in winter and struggling to dry out in summer. If you dress for the weather, hiking the headlands and watching storms roll in can be an exhilarating winter adventure along this stretch of Oregon coast. The Cape

Lookout Trail alone traces the headland for more than 2 miles and winds up at a clifftop 500 feet above the sea. There are a total of 8 miles of trails through old-growth forest in the park. Several trails offer interpretive signage noting indigenous foliage and salmon restoration efforts. Keep in mind that many of these trails are steep and slick in places. Probably safer, and equally interesting, is the 5-mile stroll along Cape Lookout State Park's sand spit, between the ocean and Netarts Bay. You should also consider taking a trip from the upper trailhead down to South Beach.

In the bay's calm waters, you'll find conditions ideal for crabbing, either by boat or from the shore. Supplies can be found in town, and several places will cook your catch for you. Clamming and fishing are other options.

If you run out of things to do (which is unlikely) and want to play tourist, Tillamook is nearby. It has a history museum, and you can take a tour of the renowned cheese factory. If you're wondering about those huge aluminum barns you can see from US 101 out in the middle of a pasture, that's the Tillamook Air Museum, which features more than 30 warbirds and actual pieces of the Hindenburg.

Cape Lookout State Park Campground

GETTING THERE

From Portland take I-405 to Exit 1D, and head west on US 26. Go 20.2 miles, and turn left onto OR 6 W. In 51.1 miles continue straight onto First Street in Tillamook. In 0.4 mile First Street turns left and becomes Birch Avenue. In 0.1 mile turn right onto OR 131 W/Netarts Highway. Drive 4.5 miles, then turn left onto Whiskey Creek Road. Drive 5.2 miles, then turn right into the park. There are signs for Cape Lookout State Park the entire way.

GPS COORDINATES: N45° 21.707'   W123° 58.153'

3

Nestucca River Recreation Area Campgrounds

Beauty ★★★★★ Privacy ★★★ Spaciousness ★★★ Quiet ★★★★ Security ★★ Cleanliness ★★★★★

The main attraction of the Nestucca River Byway is the river itself and activities that relate to it, but the coast and all its fascinations are not far away.

Not too far out there, but definitely out there, is a series of pretty, tree-covered campgrounds on the Nestucca River, remote feeling but easily accessible via the official Nestucca River National Back Country Byway. You'll have the distinct feeling that you've stumbled upon someone's private party when you arrive at these campgrounds. They're that intimate—and largely unknown to the hordes that congregate along the coast.

Four Bureau of Land Management (BLM) sites make up the Nestucca River chain of campgrounds; from east to west, they are Dovre, Fan Creek, Elk Bend, and Alder Glen. Collectively, they offer an extraordinary selection of 37 tent-camping sites spread across 9 miles of beautiful forested river frontage, so we've decided to lump them all together. Take your pick or try them all.

The campgrounds highlighted here are under the jurisdiction of the BLM's Northwest Oregon District. True to BLM campground style, the sites along the Nestucca are well-designed (albeit compact), primitive sites tucked along the banks of the river. They range in altitude from 745 feet at Alder Glen up to 1,500 feet at Dovre.

Of the four, when it comes to tent camping, Elk Bend has the most going for it. It's five walk-in sites have no fee. The three other campgrounds have either 10 or 11 campsites and a $10-per-night fee. Elk Bend stays open all year long; the others are maintained between early April and the end of November.

Elk Bend is one of several primitive campgrounds tucked away beside the Nestucca River.

KEY INFORMATION

CONTACT: Bureau of Land Management: 503-375-5646; blm.gov/visit/nestucca-river -recreation-area; blm.gov/visit/dovre -recreation-site; blm.gov/visit/fan-creek -recreation-site; blm.gov/visit/elk-bend -recreation-site; blm.gov/visit/alder-glen -recreation-site

OPEN: Year-round, depending on snow levels (not maintained and no fee December–March)

SITES: Dovre: 10; Fan Creek: 11; Elk Bend: 5; Alder Glen: 11

WHEELCHAIR ACCESS: Not designated

EACH SITE HAS: Picnic table, fire ring with grill

ASSIGNMENT: First come, first served

REGISTRATION: Self-registration on-site

AMENITIES: All: Vault toilets, solar-pumped water; Dovre also has group shelter with fire ring with grill

PARKING: At campsites; $5/additional vehicle

FEE: Elk Bend: Free; other campgrounds: $10; no fee December–March

ELEVATION: 745'–1,500'

RESTRICTIONS:

PETS: On leash only

QUIET HOURS: None specified

FIRES: In fire rings only

ALCOHOL: Permitted

OTHER: RVs up to 21'; 14-day stay limit

All campgrounds have piped water. All but Elk Bend offer wheelchair accessibility at some sites. Picnic tables and fire pits are standard issue in each campsite, and Dovre has one group shelter with its own fire pit. Alder Glen sports its own fishing pier. Garbage must be packed out of all sites.

Unless you're an avid angler, don't even think about vying for a spot along the Nestucca during the height of fall steelhead or spring and summer Chinook runs. The river is known throughout the western hemisphere for its excellent runs of both species, as well as a year-round stocked supply of cutthroat trout.

If you are a paddler, be mindful that running the river at its peak (most likely when the fish are running as well) carries the risk of getting tangled in fishing lines. (Upper portions of the Nestucca River are innavigable.) Hopefully, there's room for everyone. The rains in winter can produce a good volume of water for boaters, but the river can also achieve flood stage quickly. Use common sense, and certainly don't boat alone in peak-flow periods.

The main attraction of the Nestucca River Byway is the river itself and activities that relate to it. However, the coast and all its fascinations are not far away. Driving through the lowland meadows and farmlands on your way there, you may get sidetracked by the quaint villages that stay alive, thanks to busy US 101, but retain a few artifacts from their pre-tourism heritage. Don't blink or you'll miss Blaine, where the Nestucca River Byway takes a hard left to the west. Then comes Beaver at the byway's junction with US 101. Heading south, Hebo is home to the district office of the Siuslaw National Forest, a good place to pick up maps and information. Cloverdale calls itself "Oregon's Best Kept Secret," and I guess most people who breeze through would agree.

Hiking options are not immediately apparent at the Nestucca campgrounds. The forestlands surrounding the Nestucca River are broken up into a mix of federal, state, and private stewardship. It's difficult to know whose territory you might be stepping onto, so it is a good idea to check with either the Siuslaw National Forest, BLM, or Tillamook State Forest authorities before setting out. Recognizable hiking trails are not too far away on

Mount Hebo, where you can walk through some very old second-growth forest or clamber along an even older pioneer road converted to trail. Although there's a trail to the summit of Mount Hebo for die-hard hikers, you can also drive up for expansive views of the Nestucca Valley and west to the Pacific Ocean.

Nestucca River Recreation Area Campgrounds

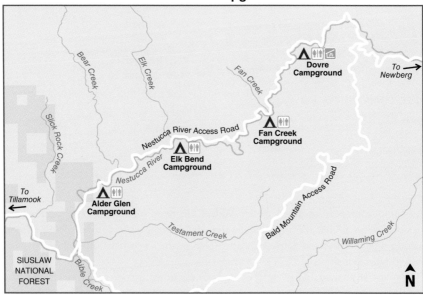

Dovre and Elk Bend Campgrounds

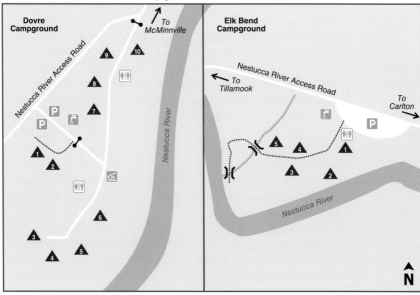

GETTING THERE

From I-5 in Portland, take Exit 294 and head south on OR 99W. Drive 27.3 miles. Turn right onto OR 47 N and drive 4.4 miles to Carlton. Turn left onto OR 47 N/W Main Street, which quickly becomes NW Meadowlake Road. Drive 12.5 miles; NW Meadowlake Road becomes Nestucca Access Road (also known as the Nestucca River Byway). Drive 7.3 more miles to the Dovre Campground on the left. There are numerous side roads that depart from the main road, so check road signs occasionally to make sure you're on the right track.

To reach Fan Creek Campground, follow the directions above to Dovre Campground, and continue another 2.7 miles; Fan Creek is on the left. To reach Elk Bend Campground, from Dovre, continue another 5.9 miles, and the campground will be on the left. To reach Alder Glen Campground, from Dovre, continue another 8.9 miles, and the campground will be on the left.

From the intersection of US 101 and OR 6 in Tillamook, drive 14.5 miles south on US 101 to Beaver. Turn left (east) onto Blaine Road and drive 6.6 miles. Continue onto Forest Service Road 85/Upper Nestucca River Road and drive 19.1 miles to the Dovre Campground on the right. Follow signs, as the road takes many jogs and twists.

To reach Fan Creek Campground, follow the directions above to FS 85/Upper Nestucca River Road, and go 16.4 miles; the campground will be on the right. To reach Elk Bend Campground, follow the directions above to FS 85/Upper Nestucca River Road, and go 13.2 miles; the campground will be on the right. To reach Alder Glen Campground, follow the directions above to FS 85/Upper Nestucca River Road, and go 10.2 miles; the campground will be on the right.

GPS COORDINATES:
  DOVRE: N45° 18.998'   W123° 28.724'
  FAN CREEK: N45° 17.478'   W123° 29.632'
  ELK BEND: N45° 16.974'   W123° 32.405'
  ALDER GLEN: N45° 15.993'   W123° 34.893'

△ Saddle Mountain State Natural Area Campground

Beauty ★★★ Privacy ★★★ Spaciousness ★★ Quiet ★★★ Security ★★ Cleanliness ★★★★

In early to mid-June, the alpine wildflowers here put on one of the most colorful shows in the region.

Want to enjoy the beach, see the mountains, and not get trampled by the crowds? Or is it one of those sweltering August days when the city feels like a sauna? Saddle Mountain is the answer. This cool green oasis is right on the way to the coast, but it's close enough to Portland to be reachable on a last-minute trip with minimal planning.

Many people hurrying along US 26 between Portland and the ocean beaches in northwestern Oregon drive right past this spot, either because they don't know about it or they're overly focused on the coast as a target.

Don't get us wrong: the Oregon coast is fabulous. If you can afford it, there are scads of wonderful places to stay—for a day, a weekend, or a week. And there are still plenty of areas that have been preserved in an undeveloped state to showcase the natural coastal beauty—we've included some great campgrounds in this very book. But if your interest is

Saddle Mountain gives you the best of both worlds: high peaks and expansive beaches within easy reach.

KEY INFORMATION

CONTACT: 503-368-5943,
   oregonstateparks.org

OPEN: April–October

SITES: 10

WHEELCHAIR ACCESS: Not designated

EACH SITE HAS: Picnic table, fire ring,
   piped water

ASSIGNMENT: First come, first served

REGISTRATION: Self-registration on-site

AMENITIES: Flush toilets (restrooms have
   running water), firewood, day-use area has
   picnic tables

PARKING: In parking lot at campground;
   $7/additional vehicle

FEE: $11

ELEVATION: 1,650'

RESTRICTIONS:

PETS: On leash only

QUIET HOURS: None specified

FIRES: In fire rings only

ALCOHOL: Permitted

OTHER: RVs must park in parking lot;
   14-day stay limit

tent camping in the purest sense—as in not another soul for miles, just you and the s'mores and the stars overhead—the Oregon coast has somewhat limited options. You'll find more possibilities for optimum peace and quiet by going farther inland to places such as Saddle Mountain State Park.

Saddle Mountain gives you the best of both worlds: it's less than 15 miles from the nearest coastal attractions of Cannon Beach and Seaside, well away from the crowded US 101 corridor, and only a 2.6-mile hike from superb views from atop the park's namesake, the highest peak in northwestern Oregon. Not a bad combination, really.

Add to that a campground (albeit primitive) for tent campers only and nearly 3,000 acres (roughly 5 square miles) of second-growth forests, fragile meadows, and clear-running creeks. You'll share the terrain with a number of woodland critters (elk have been spotted in sizable herds within the park) and a host of indigenous plant life (more than 300 species have been identified), some that for reasons not altogether clear have chosen Saddle Mountain as their preferred habitat, growing only here and nowhere else in the Oregon Coast Range.

This latter feature will be of particular interest to the weekend botanist. Saddle Mountain was a haven for certain species of plant life during the Ice Age, and much of that flora evolved in ways peculiar to the Coast Range. Today, high on the flanks of this 3,283-foot peak, plants that are not found anywhere else in the world grow. Saddle Mountain bittercress is one of these unique plants, found only on Saddle Mountain and nearby Onion Mountain. The best time to visit Saddle Mountain is early to mid-June, when the alpine wildflowers put on one of the most colorful shows in the region.

For the weekend mountaineer, Saddle Mountain Trail is a pleasantly surprising challenge, with a reward of unending views from the summit. Casual hikers will probably want to stop at the saddle just beyond the wildflower fields. The more adventurous and sure-footed in your party can continue on to the crest, but be forewarned that the path is steep and indistinct in places, making travel, as the park brochure says, "extremely treacherous" and not recommended for those who aren't in the best of shape.

Those who do make it to the top can feast on the views while enjoying a picnic lunch. To the south are Nehalem Bay and a sprinkle of small, characteristic coastal towns. Looking west, the Pacific Ocean paints a blue-green backdrop to the resort towns of Seaside and Cannon Beach, with Tillamook Head and Haystack Rock figuring prominently between them. Northward is historic Astoria, where the Columbia River meets the Pacific Ocean. Fort Clatsop is the site of Lewis and Clark's winter camp in 1805 and 1806. Snowcapped Cascade Mountain peaks to the east add a finishing touch.

The weather is not always conducive to uninterrupted vistas—or even a human presence—on the slopes of Saddle Mountain and can easily change for the worse between the time you leave your campsite and the time you finish the round-trip hike of less than 7 miles. Because the campground and the summit have an elevation differential of more than 2,000 feet, the temperature is often much warmer at the campground than at the summit, so keep that in mind as you pack. Ocean breezes can also have a chilling effect, even if the sun is bright. And in the fiercest conditions, the maritime Pacific climate has been known to dump upwards of 100 inches of rain annually, so be prepared for wet conditions anytime.

Saddle Mountain State Natural Area Campground

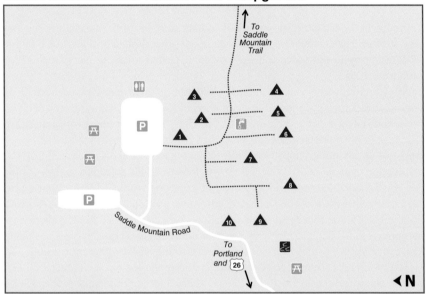

GETTING THERE

From I-405 in Portland, take Exit 1D and head west on US 26. Go 63.4 miles to Seaside, and turn right onto Saddle Mountain State Park Road (the turn is just less than a mile east of the intersection of US 26 and OR 53, also known as Necanicum Junction). Drive 7 miles to the campground. A picnic area, parking lot (self-contained RVs can park here), and the trailhead are all located here as well.

GPS COORDINATES: N45° 57.765'   W123° 41.400'

SOUTHERN COAST

Cape Blanco Lighthouse (see page 26)

Cape Blanco State Park Campground

Beauty ★★★★★ Privacy ★★★ Spaciousness ★★★★ Quiet ★★★ *(summer)* ★★★★★ *(winter)* Security ★★★★
Cleanliness ★★★★★

If you are lucky enough to snag one that backs up to the ocean, you'll have a thick forest as your buffer for the ultimate in tent-camping privacy.

Anyone who's driven along the famous US 101 knows that the entire Oregon Coast is one long necklace of windswept headlands and craggy contours, linked by a glistening thread of lowland sand dunes and tidal waterways. But the series of three capes—Blanco, Lookout, and Perpetua—is particularly stunning for its natural visual appeal, recreational opportunity, and geologic wonder. Even better: You can camp at all three.

Cape Blanco State Park is the farthest south—it's home to the southernmost of Oregon's lighthouses, and it is also the westernmost point in the state. The cape, park, reef, lighthouse, airport, and road from US 101 all bear the name Blanco, first given to the dramatic ivory cliffs that rise 200 feet above a black sand beach. In 1603, a relatively unknown Spanish explorer named Martin d'Aguilar spotted the sheer white (*blanco*, to him) cliffs and aptly dubbed them for posterity.

Watch the sun set over beautiful Cape Blanco, just steps from the campground.

KEY INFORMATION

CONTACT: 541-332-2973,
oregonstateparks.org

OPEN: Year-round

SITES: 52 with electric and water, 1 group,
1 horse camp, 1 hiker/biker camp, 4 cabins

WHEELCHAIR ACCESS: Restrooms, showers; sites A05, A06, A18, A29, A48, A49,
and A53

EACH SITE HAS: Picnic table, fire ring
with grill

ASSIGNMENT: First come, first served

REGISTRATION: Self-registration on-site

AMENITIES: Flush toilets (restrooms
have running water), hot showers,
firewood, laundry

PARKING: At campsites; $7/additional vehicle

FEE: $24

ELEVATION: 200'

RESTRICTIONS:

PETS: On leash only

QUIET HOURS: None specified

FIRES: In fire rings only

ALCOHOL: Prohibited

OTHER: 14-day stay limit

This state park covers 1,895 acres of forested headlands and wildflower fields, which flood the area with color in late spring and early summer. Yellow coneflowers, coral bells, yellow sand verbena, and northern dune tansy are the most prevalent varieties. Sitka spruce dominates in the tree department. Farther east in the coastal mountain ranges, one can find old-growth Douglas fir and the commercially prized Port Orford cedar.

The lush vegetation that stays green all year at Cape Blanco (thanks to the temperate marine climate) has been thoughtfully preserved in the campground, lending a certain air of mystery to many of the campsites. If you are lucky enough to snag one that backs up to the ocean, you'll have a thick forest as your buffer for the ultimate in tent-camping privacy. Surprisingly, considering how close the campground sits to the ocean, none seem to have water views. Only two of the cabins are situated to take in any views of the ocean, but it's only a short walk to the bluff for a panoramic vista. In a thick fog, however, make sure you know where the bluff ends and that unplanned shortcut to the beach starts! Heavy fog can prevail anytime between late October and May, but it's between December and February that the rains make their mark on Cape Blanco—and in generous supply. More than half of the area's total annual rainfall occurs in this three-month stretch. Summers (thank heavens) are generally sunny and mild. Temperatures are rarely extremely hot or cold. Shoulder seasons (March–April and September–October) bring a mixture of warm, cool, drizzly, breezy, sunny, and cloudy weather. And that's just in one day!

These shoulder seasons (part of The Discovery Season, as it's called by Oregon State Parks and Recreation) can be the perfect time to enjoy a place like Cape Blanco. The summer tourist season along the Oregon Coast—all 360 miles of it—is lovely weather-wise, and the scenery is consistently spectacular, but high season is a decidedly different kind of experience. There is little relief from the crowds, campgrounds fill up quickly (including Cape Blanco, which doesn't require reservations), and the main north–south route (US 101) can seem like one long, nearly unbroken procession of RVs and trailers.

But if summer is the only time you can get there, by all means go. You just have to be a little more creative to find the pockets of isolation. One suggestion: Try the New River paddle route just upcoast from the park in the town of Denmark. This 8-mile stretch of tidewater attracts shorebirds and migratory waterfowl. The New River is a blend of fresh waters descending from Coast Ranges and the salty Pacific, creating an interesting mix of plant and animal life. On one end of the river is undeveloped Floras Lake State Park, and at the other end are the sand dunes of Bandon. Both are equally worthy of exploration.

Another alternative is the Sixes River, which forms the northern boundary of Cape Blanco State Park. Fishing in the Sixes is best in the off-season: Chinook in the fall, sea-run cutthroat trout in spring and fall, and steelhead in the winter. There are several boat put-ins along the river east of US 101. Hikers can take their pick of varying topographies. A moderate climb up to the windswept bluff near the lighthouse offers views in all directions: north to Blacklock Point and Tower Rock, west across Blanco Reef, and south to Orford Reef. This is an excellent vantage point from which to watch gray whales on their migration path from the Arctic to Baja, California, in winter months.

Down on the beach, you can walk along portions of the Oregon Coast Trail, but keep in mind that tide levels change anywhere from 6 to 12 feet twice daily. The ultimate escape for those experienced enough to handle it is Grassy Knob Wilderness, which lies not far east in a small section of Siskiyou National Forest. Backpacking through this area is best described as bushwhacking; there are very few established trails, and the going is steep and rugged.

Cape Blanco State Park Campground

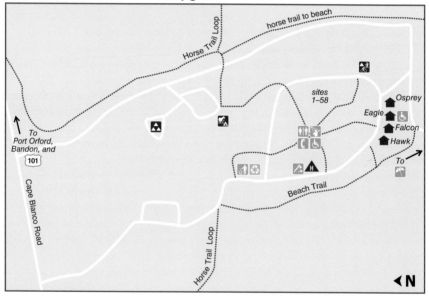

GETTING THERE

From I-5 take Exit 162 in Anlauf, and head west on OR 38. In 6.3 miles turn right to remain on OR 38. Go 50.1 miles, and turn left onto US 101 in Reedsport. In 73.1 miles turn right (west) onto Cape Blanco Road, and drive 5.2 miles into the park and to the campground.

GPS COORDINATES: N42° 50.146'   W124° 33.647'

6

Cape Perpetua Scenic Area Campground

Beauty ★★★★★ Privacy ★★ Spaciousness ★★★ Quiet ★★★★ Security ★★★★ Cleanliness ★★★★

All along this portion of the sculpted coast is an endless array of rugged inlets, crescent-shaped coves, and towering capes.

Cape Perpetua, the last of the trio of capes with campgrounds we recommend, got its name from Captain James Cook in 1778. Cook passed by as he fearlessly continued north on his fruitless search for the Pacific link to the Northwest Passage. Both Cape Perpetua and the nearby town of Yachats (pronounced "yah-hots") have long been favored vacation destinations for Oregonians who appreciate the small town's relative seclusion amid some of the coast's most awe-inspiring scenery. For some unknown reason, Yachats is often overlooked by tourists heading for the bustling centers of Newport and Florence, nearly equidistant to the north and south respectively.

Long before tourists had a road to take them anywhere in this vicinity, however, the fog-shrouded seashore and mountain slopes were the domain of coastal American Indian tribes, including Tillamook and Alsea, who fished, clammed, and hunted in blissful obscurity. Their contentment was short-lived once the Spanish, English, and Germans discovered the rich resources in the area. Along the coast and up nearby verdant river valleys, timber

Drive up to Cape Perpetua viewpoint for a dizzying panorama.

KEY INFORMATION

CONTACT: American Land & Leisure for Siuslaw National Forest, Central Coast Ranger District: 541-547-3289, www.fs .usda.gov/recarea/siuslaw/recreation /camping-cabins/recarea/?recid=42273

OPEN: Mid-March–early October

SITES: 37, 1 group

WHEELCHAIR ACCESS: Restrooms, group site, sites 34–38

EACH SITE HAS: Picnic table, fire ring with grill

ASSIGNMENT: First come, first served, or by reservation at 877-444-6777 or recreation.gov

REGISTRATION: Self-registration on-site

AMENITIES: Flush toilets, piped water, dump station, visitor center

PARKING: At campsites (back-in parking recommended); $7/additional vehicle

FEE: $26; $10 reservation fee

ELEVATION: Sea level

RESTRICTIONS:

PETS: On leash only

QUIET HOURS: None specified

FIRES: In fire rings only

ALCOHOL: Permitted

OTHER: RVs up to 22'; 14-day stay limit

mills, fish canneries, and dairy farms thrived from the late 18th century through the 20th. While there is still significant activity in these traditional industries, tourism has begun to replace them in the last several decades. Waning resources have forced residents of towns and villages all along the Oregon coast to consider alternative methods of making a living. The transition has not been easy for many of them.

While tourism has only recently seen dramatic growth, the makings for a tourism boom were first put in place in the 1930s with the extension of US 101 and the construction of the first Cape Perpetua Visitor Center by the Civilian Conservation Corps. Today's center is a renovated version of the original, and there is still evidence of the Depression-era workers' housing on the trail between the center and the beach.

The center is a good starting point before taking in the sights of this unique area. As the focal point of the surrounding piece of land known as the Cape Perpetua Scenic Area, the center offers educational exhibits and films as well as a small bookshop. Trails from the center lead off into stands of old-growth spruce in one direction and under the highway to the beach in another. All in all, there are 22 miles of hiking trails within the scenic area. Flanked by state parks on its north and south sides, a wilderness area on the east, the highly photogenic Heceta Head Lighthouse not far south, and the famed Stellar Sea Lion Caves just beyond that, Cape Perpetua Scenic Area has no lack of interesting day trips for visitors based at the campground.

Ah yes, the campground. Cape Perpetua Campground is actually two camping areas within the jurisdiction of the Siuslaw National Forest (as is the rest of the scenic area) but managed by a private contractor, American Lands & Leisure. Both are quite close to the visitor center, and the only difference between them is that one is an individual-site complex and the other accommodates groups of up to 50 people. Although privacy at the individual-site campground is painfully lacking because the sites are stretched out along the access road with little vegetation between them, at least they are situated between a creek and a cape, to give the feeling of being tucked away. Most other campgrounds in the immediate area are sprawling compounds that no one would describe as peaceful.

The campground operates mid-March–early October, but it's worth mentioning that the wild and windswept Cape Perpetua is an enormously popular whale watching spot in the wintertime. Although the campgrounds are not open, the visitor center has interpretive programs for the whale watching crowd.

If you want to witness prime examples of the geologic magnificence found at Cape Perpetua Scenic Area close up, stop at the scenic overlooks for Devil's Churn and Cook's Chasm right off the highway. The relentless movement of sea against basalt rock has formed overhanging cliffs and caves, which are pounded mercilessly at high tides by clashing currents that explode as high as 60 feet into the air. The effect is exhilarating.

All along this portion of the sculpted coast is an endless array of rugged inlets, crescent-shaped coves, and towering capes. Just south of Devil's Churn is the road up to the Cape Perpetua Viewpoint. At 800 feet above the sea, you can have a bird's-eye view of this breathtaking panorama in all directions.

Cape Perpetua Scenic Area Campground

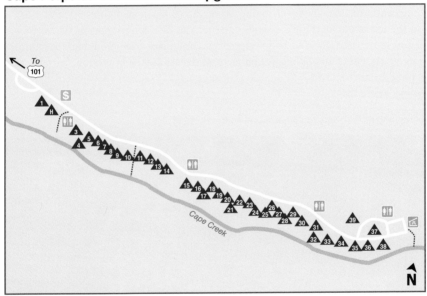

GETTING THERE

From the intersection of OR 126 and US 101 in Florence, take US 101 N and drive 23.1 miles. Turn right (east) into the park.

From the intersection of US 20 and US 101 in Newport, take US 101 S and drive 26.7 miles. Turn left (east) into the park.

GPS COORDINATES: N44° 16.942'   W124° 06.411'

7

Eel Creek Campground

Beauty ★★★★ Privacy ★★★★ Spaciousness ★★★ Quiet ★★★★ Security ★★★★ Cleanliness ★★★★

Aside from the mesmerizing appeal of the dunes, you'll find a variety of other attractions.

Welcome to the heart of the Oregon Dunes National Recreation Area. If you've never ventured into this stunning sector of the Oregon coast, prepare yourself for an experience that you will not forget.

Eel Creek is just one of many campgrounds that are clustered in the Florence/Reedsport/ Coos Bay stretch of US 101. Aside from its vegetation-lush private sites, Eel Creek's strongest selling point is the absence of off-road vehicle access to the dunes.

There are 32,000 acres of sand in the National Recreation Area, and the jeep trail stops short 1 or 2 miles south of Eel Creek, so there's space for everyone here. If you want peace and quiet as part of your dunes experience, however, make sure to avoid hiking in an area where they rent dune buggies.

Eel Creek backs up against some of the largest dunes in the 46-mile-long protected beach. Always shifting, always changing, some dunes reach as high as 600 feet. Slog your way to the top of one of these monsters and look out over a most spectacular sight—sand, sand, and more sand. Swirled and sculpted in some places, smoothed and glistening like satin in others, rising and falling like patterns of the sea frozen in motion, the pale undulations radiate under a startlingly blue August sky.

Eel Creek Campground provides an oasis among the Oregon Dunes.

KEY INFORMATION

CONTACT: Siuslaw National Forest, Oregon Dunes National Recreation Area: 541-271-6000, www.fs.usda.gov/recarea/siuslaw/recarea/?recid=42599

OPEN: Year-round

SITES: 52

WHEELCHAIR ACCESS: Not designated

EACH SITE HAS: Picnic table, fire ring with grill

ASSIGNMENT: First come, first served, or by reservation in summer at 877-444-6777 or recreation.gov

REGISTRATION: Self-registration on-site or at camp host

AMENITIES: Flush toilets, drinking water; boat launch and rentals at nearby Eel Lake

PARKING: At campsites; 2 vehicles/site

FEE: $22; $10 reservation fee

ELEVATION: Sea level

RESTRICTIONS:

PETS: On leash only

QUIET HOURS: None specified

FIRES: In fire rings only

ALCOHOL: Permitted

OTHER: RVs and trailers up to 35'; 14-day stay limit

The Pacific Ocean is solely responsible for these magnificent mounds, starting some 13,000 years ago when glacial sediment first began the tireless task of forming this section of Oregon's coast. Since then, rivers flowing out of the nearby Coast Range have also contributed their share of deposits. Seasonal patterns of wind and waves combine to add their influence to the sand's destiny, making these dunes the largest collection of active, or living, coastal sand dunes in America.

Believe it or not, from Eel Creek Campground due west to the ocean is roughly 2 miles. There are places in Oregon Dunes National Recreation Area where the dunes are as much as 3 miles wide—a stiff distance when you're making your way through soft sand. The easiest way to traverse the dunes is along any of the 30 hiking trails within the Recreation Area. It is best to keep to the trails for more noble reasons as well. This is a highly fragile ecosystem, with more than 400 different wildlife species inhabiting the dunes. Of these, 175 are birds.

Headquarters for Oregon Dunes National Recreation Area is right on US 101 at the junction with OR 38 in Reedsport. This is a well-stocked information bureau, with plenty of free guides, brochures, maps, and assorted publications. The exhibits are worth a look too. It's also a good place to compare notes with other travelers.

As with many other parts of western Oregon, late summer and early fall are prime times, weather-wise, for enjoying the dunes at their best. In winter wind speeds have been clocked as high as 100 miles an hour. Generally, the wind is more problematic than rain. Even in summer, clear skies and warm temperatures are tempered by incessant offshore breezes that often kick up little flurries of sand, which playfully tickle the ankles but can be aggravating at eye level. Sand inside a camera body can be ruinous and costly, so protect your equipment.

Aside from the mesmerizing appeal of the dunes, you'll find a variety of other attractions. The Winchester Bay area offers guided and chartered fishing options, clamming spots too numerous to mention, and a museum and lighthouse. Inland along the Umpqua River is Dean Creek Elk Viewing Area, a 923-acre preserve for free-roaming Roosevelt elk, which are native to the area. The spot also attracts a multitude of waterfowl and migratory birds, including osprey, bald eagles, and blue herons.

It's easy to confuse this campground with the RV park, which is only minutes away. Watch for signs to Eel Creek Campground about 12 miles south of Reedsport. The campground is right off US 101 but surprisingly quiet despite its close proximity to a busy thoroughfare. Heavy vegetation helps absorb traffic sounds and provides lovely secluded, sandy-bottomed tent sites. Ocean breezes help keep insects to a minimum.

Eel Creek Campground

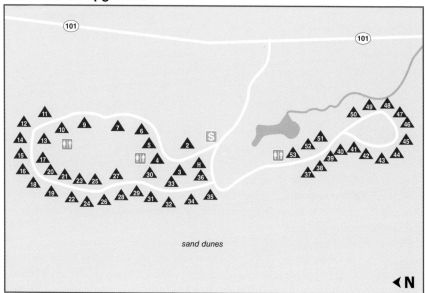

GETTING THERE

From I-5 take Exit 162 in Anlauf, and head west on OR 38. In 6.3 miles turn right to remain on OR 38. Go 50.1 miles, and turn left onto US 101 in Reedsport. Go 11 miles. Turn right (west) into the campground entrance.

From the intersection of US 101 and OR 42 south of Coos Bay, take US 101 N 21.7 miles. Turn left (west) into the campground entrance.

GPS COORDINATES: N43° 35.365'   W124° 11.228'

8

Marys Peak Campground

Beauty ★★★★ Privacy ★★★ Spaciousness ★★★ Quiet ★★★★★ Security ★★★★ Cleanliness ★★★★★

This intimate, tent-only campground sits at the highest point in Oregon's Coast.

On a clear day, the views from atop Marys Peak are unparalleled. Mount Rainier is visible to the north, Mount Hood to the east, and Mount Jefferson to the southeast. The Alsea River, favored by anglers from the Corvallis/Eugene area for its bountiful steelhead, fall Chinook, and coho salmon, fans out to the west with the glistening Pacific beyond. The Alsea is just one of a dozen major rivers sliding out of the Coast Range and into the Pacific.

At 4,097 feet, you are standing on the highest point in the Oregon Coast Range. Sir Edmund Hillary would be slightly amused at the modest elevation, but even he could appreciate that undeniable exhilaration of knowing that you are looking down on everything for as far as the eye can see.

An easy hike ends at the summit of Marys Peak, where you are rewarded with vistas of the surrounding mountains.

KEY INFORMATION

CONTACT: Siuslaw National Forest, Central Coast Ranger District: 541-563-3211, www.fs.usda.gov/recarea/siuslaw /recarea/?recid=42317

OPEN: May 1–September 30

SITES: 6

WHEELCHAIR ACCESS: Not designated

EACH SITE HAS: Picnic table, fire ring

ASSIGNMENT: First come, first served

REGISTRATION: Self-registration on-site

AMENITIES: Vault toilets, no drinking water

PARKING: At campsites

FEE: $12

ELEVATION: 4,097'

RESTRICTIONS:

PETS: On leash only

QUIET HOURS: None specified

FIRES: In fire rings only

ALCOHOL: Permitted

OTHER: No RVs or trailers; 14-day stay limit

Marys Peak (and all of the Coast Range for that matter) sits on ancient basalt that was part of the Pacific Ocean floor some 50 million–60 million years ago. Constant uplifting and shifting of tectonic plates pushes the mountain range ever upward, although the evidence of this activity is not as easily seen on Marys Peak as elsewhere in the range. The dense forest and thick soil obscure geologic evidence, making this one of the toughest areas for geologists to examine accurately.

If you are familiar with Coast Range weather, you will know that cloudless days on Marys Peak are rare indeed. Siuslaw National Forest, within which Marys Peak is located, is a coastal rain forest. That should give you some idea of the degree of wetness that pervades the place. The average annual rainfall in Siuslaw is 90 inches. There are normally as many as 180 days of measurable precipitation annually.

The driest times are late summer and early fall. But don't rule out a visit in wintertime, which can actually be quite fun if a snowfall covers the peak and makes it an ideal, untracked wonderland for cross-country skiers. The campground is closed (at a minimum) December 1–March 31, but a Northwest Forest Pass buys you the privilege to park near Connor's Camp and enjoy as much nonmotorized recreation as you can cram into a short winter day.

The same meadows that are cross-country routes in winter are flower-filled delights in the spring. Predominant year-round are the evergreens: Douglas, noble, and Pacific silver fir at the higher elevations, with an understory of sword ferns, salal, and oxalis. Stands of western hemlock grow so thickly at lower elevations that the lack of sunshine keeps the underbrush at a low ebb. To help visitors get optimum enjoyment out of the abundant foliage, a quintet of hiking trails offers various rambles around the knobby presence of Marys Peak. They range from the easy, looped Meadowedge Trail that leaves from the campground and to the top of Marys Peak to the moderate 2.4-mile East Ridge Trail through stands of old-growth Douglas fir and Sitka spruce forest to the lengthier North Ridge Trail (5.5 miles) that links Marys Peak with Woods Creek Road down. All in all, 12 miles of trails will take you through two vegetation zones, past old-growth noble fir stands, along the same route once used by sheepherders, and when conditions are right, among some of the best wildflower displays in the Coast Range.

Not all flora have enjoyed an untrammeled existence on Marys Peak, however. In the past, the U.S. Forest Service allowed disastrous quantities of timber (particularly noble fir) to be cut. A renewed effort is under way to reforest these areas, and Marys Peak Scenic Botanical Area is an experiment to preserve the noble fir and to restimulate its growth. This will not only restore the natural beauty of the area, but it will also continue to provide habitat for woodland creatures such as deer, grouse, and squirrels.

Side trips in the Marys Peak vicinity include the South Fork Alsea River Byway, the Benton County Scenic Loop, William L. Finley National Wildlife Refuge, the Willamette Floodplain, Benton County Historical Museum in Philomath and Corvallis, and Corvallis Arts Center. There's a nice bike path between Corvallis and Philomath that follows the Willamette and Marys Rivers. Mountain biking on the zillion forest roads in Siuslaw National Forest requires a very good map.

Marys Peak Campground

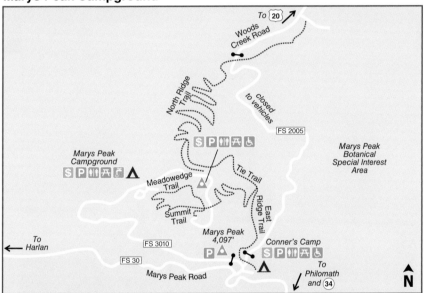

GETTING THERE

From I-5 take Exit 228, and head west on OR 34. In 9.7 miles in Corvallis, turn left onto OR 34 Bypass. In 1.1 miles continue onto US 20 W and drive 6 miles to Philomath. Turn left onto OR 34/Alsea Highway, and drive 8.9 miles. Turn right onto Marys Peak Road (which becomes Forest Service Road 3010), and drive 8.7 miles to the campground on the right.

GPS COORDINATES: N44° 30.556'   W123° 33.688'

NORTHERN CASCADES

Clouds obscure the top half of Mount Hood along the Divide Trail near Badger Lake Campground (see page 39).

photographed by Heather and Deryl Yunck (wanderingyuncks/Flickr)

9

Badger Lake Campground

Beauty ★★★★★ Privacy ★★★ Spaciousness ★★★ Quiet ★★★ *(summer)* ★★★★★ *(winter)* Security ★★★★★
Cleanliness ★★★

Hiking in this area is world-class and is really the only way to enjoy the rugged scenic beauty of the place.

Strictly for intrepid drivers and adventurous types with sturdy four-wheel-drive vehicles, Badger Lake Campground is one of those out-of-the-way places with an access road so gnarly that it just about requires being dropped in from above. (We like those, if you haven't noticed.)

The last stretch of Forest Service Road 140 (the third forest road you must navigate) is unmaintained and intended only for high-clearance vehicles. Even so, if you drove to Badger Lake right now, you would find normal, low-clearance passenger cars parked there. Who knows how they get there. You certainly can't blame campers who put forth the effort. The campground accommodates tent campers only, resulting in a noticeable lack of RVs.

Once upon a time, Badger Lake was accessible only by a steep hike up from a trailhead on OR 35. It's not entirely clear why (or if) the U.S. Forest Service considers its road access an improvement over the trail. You may wonder the same thing as you navigate the rough 10 miles on U.S. Forest Service roads from the turnoff at Bennett Pass. A good map may

Gumjuwac Creek flows into Badger Creek just northeast of the campground.
(photographed by Heather and Deryl Yunck [wanderingyuncks/Flickr])

KEY INFORMATION

CONTACT: Mount Hood National Forest, Barlow Ranger District: 541-467-2291, www.fs.usda.gov/recarea/mthood/recarea/?recid=52784

OPEN: July–September

SITES: 4 designated sites; dispersed camping around lake

WHEELCHAIR ACCESS: Not designated

EACH SITE HAS: Picnic table, fire ring with grill

ASSIGNMENT: First come, first served

REGISTRATION: Self-registration on-site

AMENITIES: Pit toilets, no piped water

PARKING: At campsites

FEE: None; Northwest Forest Pass ($5/day or $30 annually) required for parking at trailhead and day-use

ELEVATION: 4,472'

RESTRICTIONS:

PETS: On leash only

QUIET HOURS: None specified

FIRES: In fire rings only

ALCOHOL: Permitted

OTHER: No RVs or trailers; high-clearance vehicles recommended; nonmotorized boats only

---

keep you from heading off course onto even worse roads, but it won't help much with the conditions. Pick up the maps you need at the ranger station in the town of Mount Hood on OR 35 south of Hood River. If you arrive from the east via the Tygh Valley Road, stop at the Barlow Ranger Station in Dufur for information.

It's a good idea to bring along trail maps, too, as hiking in this area is world-class and is really the only way to enjoy the rugged scenic beauty of the place. The campground itself sits on the northeast edge of Badger Lake in a nonwilderness corridor adjacent to Badger Creek Wilderness, one of Oregon's smaller designated wilderness areas at only 26,000 acres. But within this tiny (by Western protected-land standards) plot are geographic transitions and climatic changes of dramatic proportions, unlike those found in any other comparably sized stretch of Oregon topography.

In this unique microcosm, forested mountains meet dusty lowlands across a span of only 12 miles, with nearly 70 inches of precipitation falling annually on the western ridges but only 20 inches in the eastern sector. Old-growth Douglas firs are gradually replaced by the unusual commingling of ponderosa pine and white oak. For some inexplicable reason, these two tree types are found together only in brief stretches along the Columbia River in Washington and along the same longitudinal line between Hood River (the city) and The Dalles in Oregon. Other arboreal examples of the concentrated, transitional diversity are mountain hemlock, lodgepole pine, and Pacific silver fir. Wildlife includes an Audubon count of 150 bird species, as well as deer and elk sightings.

For the best views of this remarkable landscape (as well as vistas of mighty Mount Hood), hike to the top of 6,525-foot Lookout Mountain. Numerous other trails lead into the backcountry to such destinations as Gumjuwac Saddle, Gunsight Butte, and Flag Point. The Divide Trail between Lookout Mountain and Flag Point looks down on the canyons of Badger Creek for glimpses of dramatic cliffs and rock formations. Wildflowers such as penstemon, Indian paintbrush, and avalanche lily are at their prime in the eastern portion of the wilderness from spring until late July, at which time the colorful displays jump to higher elevations in the west. In total, roughly 80 miles of trails traverse Badger Creek Wilderness, with connecting routes into the Mount Hood Wilderness to the north and west.

Located as it is on the eastern slopes of the Cascades at 4,472 feet, Badger Lake and its adjacent trails are usually not snow free until mid-June, but stay clear at least through mid-September. Although heavy snow prohibits travel into this high country in winter, Nordic skiers can take advantage of plowed roads from Bennett Pass southeast toward the wilderness boundary. OR 35 is kept open all winter to accommodate alpine skiers heading for Mount Hood. Boating on Badger Lake is possible if you don't lose your canoes on the way in. There's also good rainbow and brook trout fishing. The White River Paddle Route farther south along the old Barlow Road (formerly a wagon route for settlers) is another boating option.

The true beauty of Badger Lake Campground is that this remote High Cascade gem really is quite a short drive from metropolitan Portland, making it an easy weekend escape. In less than 3 hours (factoring in the slowdown on rough roads), you can enjoy a lakeside dinner on a balmy summer evening as you watch the sun sink behind Mount Hood.

Badger Lake Campground

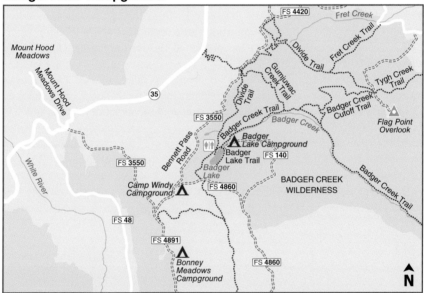

GETTING THERE

From I-84 take Exit 64 (OR 35/White Salmon/Government Camp). Head south on OR 35 and drive 32.1 miles. Take the exit toward Bennett Pass Road/Forest Service Road 3550. Turn left onto FS 3550 and drive 3.9 miles; then turn left to stay on FS 3550, and go 1 mile. Stay right to continue onto FS 4860, and drive 2.1 miles. Turn left onto FS 140 and drive 3.4 miles to the campground.

GPS COORDINATES: N45° 18.298'   W121° 33.322'

10

Beavertail Campground

Beauty ★★★★★ Privacy ★★★ Spaciousness ★★★ Quiet ★★★ *(summer)* ★★★★★ *(winter)* Security ★★★★★
Cleanliness ★★★

Untamed whitewater, steep basalt canyon walls, native trout and steelhead, and historic intrigue attract an eclectic array of recreational users.

Primitive. Desolate. Rugged. Wild. Haunting. These are a few of the adjectives that quickly come to mind when you think about the Deschutes River country. Rivière des Chutes (River of the Falls), as it was originally named by French trappers for the Hudson Bay Company, is the hallowed waterway of Central Oregon's high desert.

Flowing north out of Lava Lake just south of Mount Bachelor, the Deschutes (pronounced "deh-SHOOTS") travels toward its confluence with the mighty Columbia River under the protective aegis of state and federal legislation. This is Oregon's second-longest river, and its remarkable transformation from docile beginnings above Wickiup Reservoir to a thundering torrent downstream has prompted the separate designations of Upper Deschutes and Lower Deschutes.

Upper Deschutes (from the headwaters to Bend) has been honored with inclusion in the Oregon Scenic Waterway Program for its picturesque, recreational, and natural qualities. Its tempestuous lower half, however, often overshadows its subtle charms, which is the focus of this campground.

The Lower Deschutes River, by far the more popular of the two sections, came under wild and scenic river protection in 1988. Its untamed whitewater, steep basalt canyon walls, native trout and steelhead, and historic intrigue attract an eclectic array of recreational users from near and far. The wild and scenic status is the river's best insurance that its unspoiled existence will continue indefinitely for all to enjoy.

Basalt canyon walls loom above the Deschutes River.
(photographed by Greg Shine/Bureau of Land Management Oregon and Washington/Flickr/CC BY 2.0 [creativecommons.org/licenses/by/2.0])

KEY INFORMATION

CONTACT: Bureau of Land Management: 541-416-6700, blm.gov/visit /lower-deschutes-wild-scenic-river

OPEN: May 15–September 15 (not maintained and no fee September 16–May 14)

SITES: 17

WHEELCHAIR ACCESS: Restrooms

EACH SITE HAS: Picnic table

ASSIGNMENT: First come, first served

REGISTRATION: Self-registration on-site

AMENITIES: Vault toilets, hand-pumped water in summer, garbage service, boat launch nearby

PARKING: At campsites; 2 vehicles/site; $2/additional vehicle

FEE: Friday–Saturday, $12; Sunday–Thursday, $8; no fee September 16–May 14

ELEVATION: 900'

RESTRICTIONS:

PETS: On leash only

QUIET HOURS: 10 p.m.–6 a.m.

FIRES: Not allowed June–mid-October; see blm.gov for details.

ALCOHOL: Permitted

OTHER: Driving on vegetation not allowed; no fishing from boats

Today, Beavertail Campground is one of several minimally developed sites along the eastern bank of the Lower Deschutes that are provided in classic, barely-there Bureau of Land Management (BLM) style.

The BLM knew what it was doing when it created Beavertail. Views across the water from the riverside compound encompass some of the Lower Deschutes's most spectacular basalt canyon walls. Cedar Island is just downstream, so named for a misplaced stand of incense cedar, which typically grows farther west in the Cascades. Wildlife abounds in this area. Be sure to keep your eyes peeled for osprey, river otters, and bighorn sheep along the bands of cliffs. Photographers, grab your gear and find a comfortable spot among the shore grasses. The kayaks and rafts will be bobbing around the bend any minute.

Speaking of boating, the 51-mile trip from Maupin to the Columbia via the Deschutes requires a permit (available at local outfitters in Central Oregon, or on the web at boater pass.com). The BLM website is full of information for boaters planning a trip on the Lower Deschutes and might be a good place to start your trip even before leaving the house. It includes detailed maps as well as information on how to get a boating permit. For more experienced boaters, there is one Class IV rapid (Oak Springs), as well as many less technical runs for novices.

One rapid is in a class all by itself. It's known as Sherars Falls (pronounced "sheerers"). This Class VI rapid is a mandatory portage for all boaters. The falls are still in use today by members of the Confederated Tribes of Warm Springs, who dipnet for trout and spawning salmon from rickety platforms that teeter precariously over the raging spillway below. It's an awesome sight to behold: anglers pulling up a fish about every 10 minutes and clubbing it senseless with one swift bash of a wooden stick, lashing the net back into position, then gutting the catch at lightning speed and carefully packing each in a blanket laden with ice. Except for the ice, this technique has been practiced the same way for centuries.

The climate in this rugged wildwater backcountry is, as you may have guessed, as extreme as the terrain. Summers can be very hot (in the 90s and 100s), while winters generally drop below freezing. The BLM lands in this area are open all year, so make sure you have all the appropriate emergency supplies, depending on your choice of season. Gusty winds and sudden thunderstorms are commonplace. This is a spare campground with the typical scraggly vegetation of the high desert such as small juniper trees, sagebrush, and native grasses. In other words, there are no towering evergreens to protect you. The car may be the best place to dive if the elements get out of control.

The road that accesses Beavertail and all other BLM dispersed and managed sites is officially known as the Lower Deschutes National Back Country Byway. But it is commonly labeled Deschutes River Access Road on maps. More information about the scenic byway can be obtained on the byways.org website. This thoroughfare can be quite crowded in summer, especially on weekends. Use particular caution if you choose to explore by mountain bike; gravel goes flying as cars career past.

Beavertail Campground

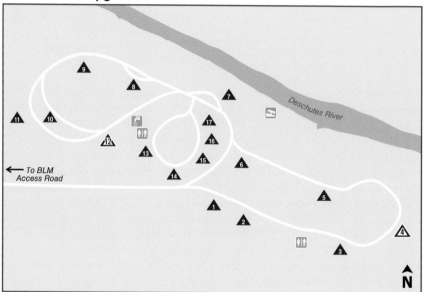

GETTING THERE

From I-84 take Exit 87 in The Dalles, and head south on US 197/US 30. In 0.2 mile turn left onto US 197, and go 28.1 miles. Turn left onto OR 216, and go 8.4 miles. Turn left onto BLM Access Road, which is a gravel road; there is a large BLM sign here. Drive 9.8 miles to the campground entrance of Beavertail Campground on the left. Turn left, and go 0.6 mile to the campground.

From the intersection of US 97 and US 197 south of Maupin, head north on US 197, and go 21.2 miles. Turn right onto Bakeoven Road (just before the bridge over the Deschutes River). Drive just 0.3 mile, then turn left onto BLM Access Road/Deschutes River Road. Drive 8 miles to a three-way stop; turn right onto OR 216 E and drive 0.5 mile. Turn left onto a gravel road, which is the continuation of the BLM Access Road (there is a large BLM sign here). Drive 9.8 miles to the campground entrance of Beavertail Campground on the left. Turn left, and go 0.6 mile to the campground.

GPS COORDINATES: N45° 20.155'   W120° 57.137'

11

Camp Creek Campground

Beauty ★★★★ Privacy ★★★ Spaciousness ★★★ Quiet ★★★ Security ★★★ Cleanliness ★★★★

You won't even realize that you're a stone's throw away from civilization once you set up your tent at one of the creekside sites.

Tired of driving forever on rough forest roads just to find a place to set up camp? Then check out Camp Creek. You can't beat the convenience of this campground, located directly off US 26 right in the heart of the Mount Hood National Forest.

    While the campground itself doesn't have supplies (except firewood, which you can buy from the camp host), it's a short distance to the small mountain towns of Zigzag and Government Camp. You won't even realize that you're a stone's throw away from civilization once you set up your tent at one of the creekside sites, which provide white noise as a pleasant, natural backdrop. The shade of the Douglas fir trees and the rushing creek give you the feeling of having gotten away from it all. Although, as with many of the area campgrounds, it tends to get a little crowded. The beauty of Camp Creek Campground is that the sites are relatively spacious, so you won't feel like you're on top of your neighbor. In one of our favorite sites, there is a seat carved out of a tree trunk where you can sit and enjoy a private view

An easy hike from Camp Creek Campground leads to Little Zigzag Falls.

KEY INFORMATION

CONTACT: Mount Hood National Forest, Zigzag Ranger District: 503-328-0909, www.fs.usda.gov/recarea/mthood /recarea/?recid=53346

OPEN: Late May–early September

SITES: 25

WHEELCHAIR ACCESS: Not designated

EACH SITE HAS: Picnic table, fire ring

ASSIGNMENT: First come, first served, or by reservation at 877-444-6777 or recreation.gov

REGISTRATION: With camp host

AMENITIES: Vault toilets, hand-pumped water, firewood

PARKING: At campsites; $8/additional vehicle

FEE: Single $19, premium $21; $2/night holidays and holiday weekends; $10 reservation fee

ELEVATION: 2,200'

RESTRICTIONS:

PETS: On leash only

QUIET HOURS: None specified

FIRES: In fire rings only

ALCOHOL: Permitted at campsites only

OTHER: RVs up to 22'

of the moon lighting up the creek below. The Civilian Conservation Corps constructed the campground in 1936. Some features from this era remain, such as several stone fireplaces.

Only 20 miles east of Portland, Mount Hood National Forest totals 1,067,043 acres, of which 189,200 are in designated wilderness areas. Mount Hood Wilderness, the largest area, encompasses the summit and upper slopes of its namesake peak. The forest is laced with hiking trails, many within a few miles of Camp Creek. In fact, the 1.6-mile Still Creek Trail starts in the campground; the U.S. Forest Service website describes it as "simply a pleasant forest trail . . . there is a short section of decked trail that goes through a wet cedar grove." Fishing, berry-picking, bird-watching, bicycling, and mushroom-hunting are also popular activities in the area.

Hidden Lake Trail, inside the Mount Hood Wilderness area, departs from a trailhead off FS 2639 (Kiwanis Camp Road), which intersects OR 26 about 5 miles east of the hamlet of Rhododendron. Along the path you'll spot many of the flowering shrubs for which the town is named (blossoming in profusion in June) as you ascend to a forested lake. A round-trip to the terminus (beyond the lake) totals 10 miles. The easier 0.6-mile Little Zigzag Falls Trail also departs from FS 2639 to follow Little Zigzag Creek to its namesake falls. The best hike in the area is the Mirror Lake Trail, just 7 miles up US 26; follow it 1.5 miles gradually uphill to a lovely lake with a view of Mount Hood, or go another 2 miles up to the top of Tom Dick and Harry Ridge, where the view is astounding. You can get the latest local trail information by visiting mthood.info, which will give you details on snow conditions, recent trail maintenance, and permit requirements.

The Zigzag Ranger District also sponsors several wildflower hikes during the summer. The popular Top Spur Trail leads through flower-cloaked meadows to the crest of Bald Mountain and then on to McNeil Point, and the Trillium Lake Trail traverses colorful fields at the water's edge. Contact the district at 503-622-3191 for guided-hike schedules and for additional information on Mount Hood's many trails. Note that trailhead parking requires a Northwest Forest Pass ($5 per day or $30 annually).

If you want a close-up view of the 11,237-foot Mount Hood, Oregon's tallest mountain, take the 6-mile winding drive up to historic Timberline Lodge, which sits (as the name indicates) right at the timberline, where the trees give way to rock; it offers restaurants and hiking trails with a great view of the mountain and some fine beverages.

Overall, Camp Creek is a great base camp for anything you might want to do in the Mount Hood area, and with its combination of convenience and great scenery, it's one of the top spots in this popular region. Consequently, you may want to reserve a creekside site if you plan to be here during a holiday weekend, or any sunny summer weekend for that matter, as those are the best plots of the bunch.

Camp Creek Campground

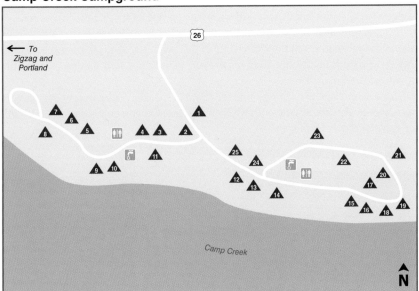

GETTING THERE

The campground entrance is about 4.8 miles east of Zigzag.

From I-205 N in Portland, take Exit 19 (US 26/Powell Boulevard). Turn right onto US 26 E and drive 40 miles. Turn right into the campground.

From I-205 S in Portland, take Exit 19 (Division Street/US 26 E). Turn left onto SE Division Street, and drive 0.9 mile; turn right onto SE 112th Avenue and drive 0.5 mile. Turn left onto SE Powell Boulevard/US 26 E and drive 39.2 miles. Turn right into the campground.

From I-84 take Exit 64 in Hood River, and head south on US 30. Go 0.4 mile and continue onto OR 35 S. Go 38.2 miles, and merge onto US 26 W. Go 9.5 miles, and turn left into the campground.

GPS COORDINATES: N45° 18.275'   W121° 52.025'

12

Elk Lake Campground

Beauty ★★★★★ Privacy ★★★★ Spaciousness ★★★★★ Quiet ★★★★★ Security ★★★ Cleanliness ★★★★

This campground may be tough to get to, but once you're there, it makes for a terrific base camp while you enjoy the region's recreational options.

Hugging the southern boundary of Bull of the Woods Wilderness, peaceful Elk Lake (not to be confused with the Elk Lake near Mount Bachelor) is named for the huge herds of elk (you guessed it) that once grazed in this area. It lies in the subalpine shadow of Battle Ax Mountain, Mount Beachie, and Gold Butte, and is a classic Cascade escape that probably remains so because the U.S. Forest Service insists on not improving the access road. (Perhaps the ill maintenance is intentional, but on the other hand, it may be a matter of funds.) Elk Lake Campground sits at the western tip of this peanut-shaped lake and is accessible by following the road along the north side of the lake to the short spur that drops down off the main road to the left.

Elk Lake's campsites are strung along the shore of the lake. Tall stands of Douglas fir and western hemlock share the land with white fir, birches, Oregon grape, ferns, and trillium to

Remote Elk Lake makes an excellent base for hikes in the area.

KEY INFORMATION

CONTACT: Willamette National Forest, Detroit Ranger District: 503-854-3366, www.fs.usda.gov/recarea/willamette/recarea/?recid=4218

OPEN: July–October, depending on snow levels

SITES: 17

WHEELCHAIR ACCESS: Not designated

EACH SITE HAS: Picnic table, fire ring with grill

ASSIGNMENT: First come, first served

REGISTRATION: None

AMENITIES: Vault toilets, primitive boat launch; no piped water, no garbage service

PARKING: At campsites and in general parking area (a short walk to some campsites); $5/additional vehicle

FEE: $10

ELEVATION: 3,700'

RESTRICTIONS:

PETS: On leash only

QUIET HOURS: None specified

FIRES: In fire rings only

ALCOHOL: Permitted

OTHER: High-clearance vehicles recommended; no camping within 500 feet of Elk Lake; no motorized boating; ATV use is allowed only to enter and leave the campground; 14-day stay limit; no chain saws

offer a prime collection of natural cover. In early July, pink-blossomed rhododendrons seem somehow out of place in this rugged, woodsy setting.

This campground may be tough to get to, but once you're there, it makes for a terrific base camp while you enjoy the region's recreational options. At the top of the list is hiking into Bull of the Woods Wilderness, which is home to one of western Oregon's few remaining old-growth forests. From Beachie Saddle (about a mile west of the campground on FS 4697), trailheads strike out for Battle Ax Mountain to the north (into the wilderness) and Mount Beachie to the south. This section of FS 4697 is not recommended for any motor vehicles; consider this a warm-up for the steep 2-mile and 1.5-mile grunts up Battle Ax and Beachie, respectively. You will be greeted, however, by views that are well worth the effort. A less strenuous hike follows Elk Lake Creek northeast into Bull of the Woods Wilderness from a trailhead near where the creek feeds its namesake.

For extended trips into the wilderness backcountry, take the trail that leaves very near the campground spur road. In 1998 a sizable chunk of Bull of the Woods Wilderness was annexed to help create adjoining Opal Creek Wilderness, so be sure you have a current map showing both areas.

If you are thinking Elk Lake might be a nice spot to take in lazy kayaking or canoeing, you're right. Anyone foolhardy enough to drag a boat into this remote locale deserves to be rewarded (or psychoanalyzed). An undeveloped put-in accommodates inflatable rafts, kayaks, canoes, and other small, nonmotorized craft. Pick up a fishing permit at the general store in Detroit if you have thoughts of angling for your dinner. For either boating or fishing, don't overlook little Dunlap Lake (named for an early prospector), which is hidden from view about a mile before you get to Elk Lake. U.S. Forest Service roads also await exploration if you have the foresight to bring your mountain bike along. Test your skill downhill on the 2-mile "riverbed" and pedal on up FS 4696 (to the left) to Gold Butte Lookout. The views of mountain peaks from this formerly manned fire lookout are staggering on a clear day— north to Mount Hood, east to Mount Jefferson, south to Mount Washington. The lookout is another impressive example of the work of the Civilian Conservation Corps, which built so many of Oregon's enduring outdoor facilities in the 1930s. During World War II, the lookout was temporarily pressed into service as an aircraft warning station, staffed around the clock. These days, you can rent the place in summer (though you'll need to reserve it many months in advance, like most of the rentable fire lookout towers in Oregon). It's a particular hit with stargazers, as there's scarcely any ambient light to interfere with the view.

Farther up FS 46 is Breitenbush Hot Springs, worth a dip for tired muscles.

Elk Lake Campground

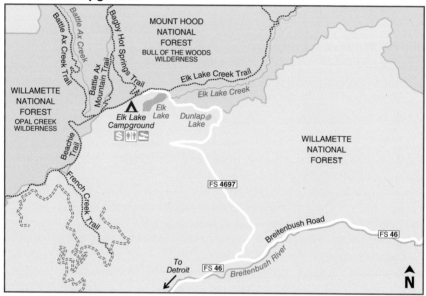

GETTING THERE

From I-5 take Exit 253 in Salem (OR 22 E/OR 99E/Detroit Lake). Head east on OR 22, and drive 48.7 miles to Detroit. Turn left onto Forest Service Road 46/Breitenbush Road and drive 4.4 miles. Turn left onto an unnamed road, and then make an almost immediate right onto FS 701. Drive 0.6 mile, then turn left onto FS 4697 and drive 6.6 miles. Turn left into the campground.

GPS COORDINATES: N44° 49.346' W122° 07.669'

13

⛺ Oxbow Regional Park Campground

Beauty ★★★★ Privacy ★★★ Spaciousness ★★★★ Quiet ★★★ Security ★★★★★ Cleanliness ★★★★

It's easy to lose yourself in the spaciousness and ramble to your heart's content.

Oxbow Regional Park is a prime example of what a metropolitan park can and should be. An easy 20 miles from downtown Portland, the park is an amazing blend of recreational diversity, scenic delight, and environmental consciousness. The grounds are a sprawling 1,000 acres of dense forests, grassy clearings, Sandy River frontage, and sheer canyon walls. Old-growth forest covers 180 acres. Native salmon spawn within 0.25 mile of camping areas on the Sandy River, known as the top-rated winter steelhead stream in Oregon. Wildlife abounds in the park, with more than 200 native plant varieties, 100 bird species, nearly 40 different mammals, and an interesting assortment of reptiles and water-dwelling creatures. The park employs a full-time naturalist year-round, who is busiest in summer, thanks to a heavy schedule of public and private programs.

Campers enjoy a choice of plenty of campsites and new restroom buildings, with the ultimate in camping comfort: flush toilets, hot showers, heated bathroom floors, and hot-air hand dryers. In 2018 the park added 17 new campsites (partly to replace 10 sites that had washed out), two playgrounds, and a welcome center. It's almost better than home—but with all the other rustic charms and natural beauty that make this such a great park.

Over the years, park staff has worked to improve the privacy between sites with natural vegetation and cedar fences. It's music to the ears of tent campers everywhere when peace and quiet become a priority.

The first order of business after finding your spot may be to explore the trails on foot. Roughly 15 miles of trail follow the Sandy River and wind throughout the park. It's easy to

The spacious, kid-friendly Oxbow Regional Park is only 20 miles from Portland.

KEY INFORMATION

CONTACT: 503-663-4708, oregonmetro.gov/parks/oxbow-regional-park

OPEN: Year-round

SITES: 74 (10 for RVs), 2 group

WHEELCHAIR ACCESS: Restrooms; sites 8, 18, 26, and 67

EACH SITE HAS: Picnic table, freestanding barbecue grill, lantern pole

ASSIGNMENT: First come, first served, or by reservation at 800-452-5687 or reserveamerica.com

REGISTRATION: Daily fee collected each evening at campsite; vehicle fee at entrance

AMENITIES: Flush toilets, hot showers, heated restroom floors; firewood, playground, boat ramp, equestrian area, interpretive programs

PARKING: At campsites; 2 vehicles/site; $5/vehicle

FEE: $22; $8 reservation fee

ELEVATION: Sea level

RESTRICTIONS:

PETS: Not permitted

QUIET HOURS: 10 p.m.–7 a.m.

FIRES: In fire rings only, subject to seasonal restrictions; no gathering firewood

ALCOHOL: Prohibited

OTHER: RVs up to 35'; no hookups; no ATVs; no guns or fireworks; 6 people/site; 14-day stay limit; entrance gate locked sunset–6:30 a.m.

lose yourself in the spaciousness and ramble to your heart's content with no other thought than to see how many of the birds on the park's list (available at the office) you can identify. Wander into the old-growth forest and contemplate a summer idyll. There's a small waterfall nearby to enhance your poetic musings. Slip through the underbrush to a sun-warmed curve in the river and wriggle your toes in the sand. Even at the height of the summer season, you'll be amazed at how quickly you can find seclusion.

For a different perspective of the trail system, the park allows horses on most of the pathways. There are designated equestrian unloading areas, and trailhead markers indicate those that are restricted.

Fishing and boating activities are undeniably central to the popularity of Oxbow Park and Sandy River. Most often they go hand in hand. There are very few times of the year when anglers won't find a reason to cast their lines into the broad and shallow waters. Along with its preeminent status as a steelheader's delight, the Sandy also sports healthy quantities of coho, fall and spring Chinook, and summer steelhead. Check with the park office for fishing regulations on the Sandy, as they differ from those of other Oregon rivers.

Recreational boating on this section of the Sandy is limited to nonmotorized craft, thanks to the recent state and federal designations of the Wild and Scenic Sandy River. Above Oxbow Regional Park, and depending on flow levels, there are Class III and IV whitewater rapids for experienced kayakers, rafters, and canoeists to enjoy. A popular run is the 6 miles between Dodge Park and Oxbow, affording exclusive views of this section of the river gorge. Downstream from Oxbow to Lewis and Clark State Recreation Site is a pleasant drift trip with gentle ripples and refreshing pools for an occasional dip. Additional river and boat-rental information is available at the park office.

If you're interested in exploring beyond the park's boundaries, Oxbow can be the starting point for a couple of scenic drives that allow you to see a lot with minimal time commitments. The shorter of the two is the route along Crown Point Highway, named for the 700-foot piece of basalt that spires above the Columbia River. Crown Point Vista House, with its information center, is well worth the visit, not to mention the staggering views afforded from its lofty perch.

The second route takes you southeast on US 26 through the Sandy River lowlands, around Mount Hood, north to Hood River on OR 35, and back along I-84 to Exit 18 at Lewis and Clark State Recreation Site. This is roughly 150 miles of non-stop scenery, with the snowy peak of Mount Hood as the focal point most of the way. From Hood River back to Oxbow, the changing landscape of the Columbia River Gorge unfolds around each bend in the road.

Oxbow is a well-managed park that gives foremost consideration to the interests of its visitors. There is even a ranger on duty in the park 24 hours per day in the event of an emergency.

Oxbow Regional Park Campground

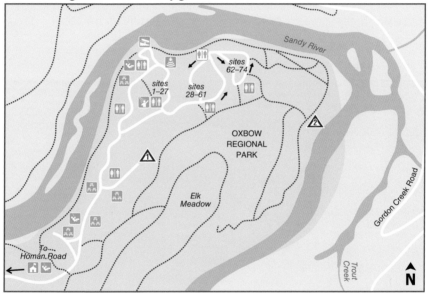

GETTING THERE

From I-84 in Portland, take Exit 16 (238th Drive/Wood Village). Head south on NE 238th Drive (from eastbound, a right turn; from westbound, a left turn), and drive 2.6 miles (during which NE 238th will become NE 242nd/NE Hogan Drive). Turn left onto NE Division Street and drive 2 miles, then turn right onto SE Division Drive. In 1.4 miles turn right onto SE Oxbow Drive; from here, there will be signs to the park. (The road winds around a bit, and there are several spots where it is easy to make a miscalculated turn.) Drive 2.2 miles, then turn left onto SE Hosner Road, and drive 1.4 miles. Turn right into the park entrance and drive 2.5 miles to the campground; it's a sharp and curving drop down into the gorge.

GPS COORDINATES: N45° 29.797'   W122° 17.427'

14

⚠ Silver Falls State Park Campground

Beauty ★★★★ Privacy ★★★ Spaciousness ★★★ Quiet ★★★ Security ★★★★ Cleanliness ★★★★

The park includes more than 25 miles of hiking trails, 14 miles of horse trails, and several biking paths, so there will be plenty to keep you busy.

If you're looking for a weekend destination where you can see it all in one place, Silver Falls State Park is the place to go. As the largest state park in Oregon, the 8,700-acre Silver Falls is renowned for its hiking. The 7-mile Silver Creek Canyon Trail (also known as Trail of Ten Falls) traverses a lush forest floor covered with Oregon grape, salal, and sword ferns beneath second-growth fir, hemlock, and cedar trees.

The trail follows the north and south forks of Silver Creek, passing 10 waterfalls en route. It runs behind several tall falls and along the edges of others—you'll definitely want a rain jacket, as the approach to each of the falls essentially means walking through a

The Trail of Ten Falls at Silver Falls State Park is a great way to cool off on a hot day.

KEY INFORMATION

CONTACT: 503-873-8681, 800-551-6949, oregonstateparks.org

OPEN: Year-round; tent sites (those without electric) closed October 31–April 30

SITES: 97 (52 with electric)

WHEELCHAIR ACCESS: Restrooms, sites 2 and 4

EACH SITE HAS: Picnic table, fire ring

ASSIGNMENT: First come, first served, or by reservation at 800-452-5687 or reserveamerica.com

REGISTRATION: At park entrance

AMENITIES: Flush toilets, hot showers

PARKING: At campsites and at park entrance; 1 vehicle/site; $7/additional vehicle

FEE: $19; $8 reservation fee

ELEVATION: 250'

RESTRICTIONS:

PETS: On leash only (dogs not allowed on the Trail of Ten Falls)

QUIET HOURS: None specified

FIRES: In fire rings only

ALCOHOL: Permitted at campsites only

OTHER: 14-day stay limit

tiny monsoon. Bring your camera along for the South Falls, the largest of the falls, which plummets 177 feet and backs up to a tunnel through which visitors can view the cascade. If you feel like you've seen it before, you probably have: Silver Falls is one of the most-photographed places in the state. Hiking the entire circuit can take at least 3 hours, so pack a picnic lunch and make an all-day excursion of it. To preserve its primitive nature, the trail is uninterrupted by picnic tables, shelters, or restrooms, but there are plenty of these scattered around the main parking lot.

If you want to let someone else do the walking, horse rentals are also a popular activity in this park, where you can arrange 1-hour guided tours. The park includes more than 25 miles of hiking trails, 14 miles of horse trails, plus several biking paths, so there will be plenty to keep you busy (make sure to get a handy map at the park entrance). Wildlife you may spot while on the trail includes blacktail deer, black bears, and cougars, although beavers and chipmunks are more likely.

If you feel like taking a dip, there is a developed beach on the east shore of Silver Creek. There is no lifeguard on duty; restrooms, a snack bar, and a playground are located nearby.

Silver Falls State Park took its name from the former town of Silver Falls City, population 200, which stood where the South Falls parking lot now lies. (It officially became a park in the early 1930s.) Evidence of the town's main source of income—logging—remains in some of the park's large cedar stumps—notches from springboards the loggers wedged into the trees' trunks to cut them. At the historic South Falls Lodge, you can enjoy a posthike latte and take a glimpse back into history through the collection of old logging photos and antique tools. The lodge, originally designed as a restaurant, was constructed by the Civilian Conservation Corps and Works Project Administration in the 1930s, closed in the late 1950s, and restored pursuant to its placement on the National Register of Historic Places in 1983. All of the more than 100 pieces of furniture in the lodge was crafted from two myrtlewood logs 5 feet in diameter and 40 feet long.

The nearby town of Silverton is home to the Silverton Historical Museum, a 1908 home that contains even more photographs and artifacts from the area's farming and logging history. Visit in July to catch the annual Historic Silver Falls Day festival, commemorating Al Faussett's 1928 plunge over South Falls in a canvas canoe. Present-day Faussett family members converge at the falls, along with hundreds of visitors who are treated to a newsreel of the actual event, plus live music, food, and family fun.

While many campgrounds are mere jumping-off points for nearby attractions, Silver Falls is one area that neatly encompasses all activities in its boundaries. Cabins are also available for rent, and there are several group-camping sites as well. Although the park tends to get a little crowded because it's so popular—and long has been, even decades before the first land was deeded to the state for a park—it's also quite easy to lose the crowds because of its sheer size.

Despite the area's name, no one has struck it rich mining silver, gold, or any other ore here, but the park's natural wonders are a perfect example of our most precious commodities.

Silver Falls State Park Campground

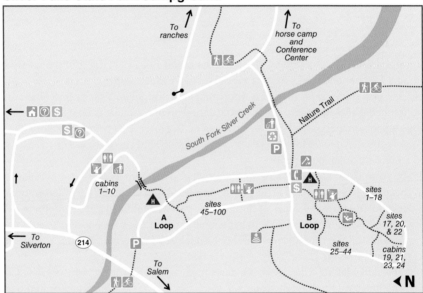

GETTING THERE

From I-5 near Salem, take Exit 253 (OR 22/OR 99E/Detroit Lake). Head east on OR 22, and drive 7.7 miles to Exit 9 (Shaw/Aumsville). Turn right onto First Street/Shaw Highway and drive 0.9 mile, then stay to the right to continue onto Brownell Drive and drive 1.3 miles. Brownell Drive becomes OR 214 N; continue straight another 11.9 miles, into the park. You will turn right toward the campground registration booth.

GPS COORDINATES: N44° 52.420'   W122° 39.055'

15

Summit Lake Campground

Beauty ★★★★ Privacy ★★★★ Spaciousness ★★★★★ Quiet ★★★★★ Security ★★★★★ Cleanliness ★★★★★

Recreational opportunities abound, with two scenic byways to explore, the Wild and Scenic Clackamas River to admire, trout-stocked lakes to tackle, and endless mountain ridges to wander.

The name is a bit misleading, as there is no sense of having reached the top of something when you get to Summit Lake. (There is a lake, though.) But once you're here, you'll feel like you're on top of the world, simply because you managed to find this wonderfully basic yet delightful spot far from the Timothy Lake crowds.

Summit Lake is on the order of Rujada (see page 85)—a great place to visit when you don't have a lot of time and don't want a heavy agenda. Unlike Rujada, Summit Lake is underdeveloped and primitive, with mostly walk-in sites either anchored by the shoreline or on a slight inland incline with a lake view.

Access to Summit Lake is almost too easy, which is what makes the lack of crowds so surprising. It could be that the magnetic draw of Timothy Lake, with its eye-popping views of Mount Hood, is all it takes to divert impressionable campers. It also could be that those who value a sublime place like Summit Lake aren't about to share it with others. The most plausible theory of all is that most people drive way too fast to notice the very small,

Every campsite features a view of Summit Lake. *(photographed by Kacy Matthews-Hall)*

KEY INFORMATION

CONTACT: Mount Hood National Forest, Zigzag Ranger District: 503-622-3191, www.fs.usda.gov/recarea/mthood /recarea/?recid=53498

OPEN: June–early September

SITES: 8

WHEELCHAIR ACCESS: Not designated

EACH SITE HAS: Picnic table, fire ring with grill

ASSIGNMENT: First come, first served

REGISTRATION: Self-registration on-site

AMENITIES: Vault toilets, piped water, garbage service

PARKING: In parking area; $8/additional vehicle

FEE: $17

ELEVATION: 4,200'

RESTRICTIONS:

PETS: On leash only

FIRES: In fire rings only

ALCOHOL: Permitted

OTHER: RVs up to 16'; no hookups; 14-day stay limit; nonmotorized boats only

dark-brown wooden sign engulfed in foliage on the Oregon Skyline Road (also known as Forest Service Road 42), pointing the way to Summit Lake down FS 141.

Whatever the reasons, Summit Lake shows up on detailed topographic maps as the tiniest blue slash alongside the Skyline Road, and those of us who have discovered its charms hope the campground retains its rustic, untrammeled character.

Here's a simple lesson in how to enjoy Summit Lake: Drive the mile of decent gravel off the Skyline Road down FS 141, park the car in the group-parking area, take a short walk along one of the camp trails, pick the spot of your choice (you may not have as many choices on the weekend), and then unload the car. Total time from turning off Skyline Road: 20 minutes.

Summit Lake will appear on your left as you drive along FS 141, so enjoy the preview. Campsites 1 and 2 are the only drive-in sites, but they're not necessarily the best sites because they have very little privacy and are opposite the parking area for the walk-in sites. They're likely to get noisy and busy with engines starting, doors slamming (there should be a camp rule against this), and gear being transported.

Go for sites 4 and 5 if you can. These are the farthest from the parking area, so toting a lot of stuff can be a bit of a drag, and you have to pass the other campsites getting there. (Keep to the trail; cutting through other campsites is a major camping faux pas.) Sites 4 and 5 offer the best vantage for enjoying lake views and those early-morning sunrises. Site 3 isn't all bad, but it sits fairly near the parking area. Sites 7 and 8 sit back from the lake but are bounded on all sides by the trails that lead through the campground, perhaps an annoying element when children chase each other through the underbrush oblivious to your tent nearby. Site 6 sits alone up a small grade and has the best overview of the lake and the other campsites.

In general, the sites are spacious with a smattering of foliage in between to soften the views, but one would not describe the underbrush as lush or the campsites as shrouded. A tent positioned in the right way can do a lot to act as a curtain. What these sites lack in privacy, however, they make up for by being spaced well apart. Each has the basic amenities—picnic table and fire ring with grill—and they share a modern vault toilet near the parking area. Garbage services are a notable plus.

The Oregon Skyline Road, which passes by Summit Lake, cuts a midelevation swath between the dense Mount Hood National Forest on its western flank and the rolling ridges of the Warm Springs Indian Reservation to the east. It ultimately meets up with FS 46, which continues northward as Clackamas River Road and becomes Breitenbush Road to the south before its junction with OR 22 at Detroit.

Recreational opportunities abound, with two scenic byways to explore, the Wild and Scenic Clackamas River to admire, trout-stocked lakes to tackle, and endless mountain ridges to wander. Bring a good map, a set of binoculars, a comfortable pair of boots, and however much time you can spare. You may not accomplish everything on this trip, but it's not too far away, so you can come back soon.

Summit Lake Campground

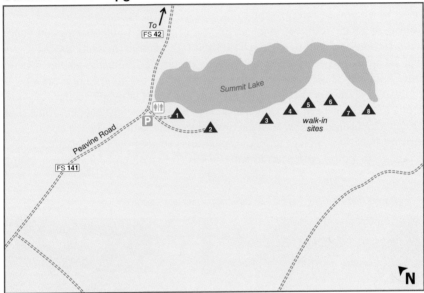

GETTING THERE

From the intersection of US 26 and OR 35 on the south side of Mount Hood National Forest (just past Government Camp), take US 26 E and drive 8.6 miles. Turn right onto Forest Service Road 42/Skyline Road and drive 8.3 miles. Stay left to continue on FS 42 another 4.9 miles. Turn right onto FS 141/Peavine Road (the sign is nearly hidden by vegetation, so watch your mileage). Drive 0.8 mile to Summit Lake on your left.

GPS COORDINATES: N45° 01.960'   W121° 47.445'

⚠ Whispering Falls Campground

Beauty ★★★★ Privacy ★★★★ Spaciousness ★★★ Quiet ★★★ Security ★★★ Cleanliness ★★★★

Choose the right spot here and you'll feel like you're completely on your own, in a secret hideout in the woods.

One of a handful of campgrounds strung along OR 22, Whispering Falls nestles up against the North Santiam River, with sites tucked discreetly away among tall trees and lush vegetation. It's especially pretty in the fall, when the changing leaves add a splash of bright color and give the whole area a warm, subtle glow.

Whispering Falls is one of those places you drive past a million times on your way between Detroit Lake and Bend. You'll notice it right around the same time you're wondering, yet again, just exactly how to correctly pronounce the name *Idanha*. (We're still not sure.) But why choose this campground over any of the others along the way? Well, here's the secret: Choose the right spot here and you'll feel like you're completely on your own, in a secret hideout in the woods by a river, where there just happens to be running water and a bathroom nearby. We won't reveal the source of this information, except to say that it's always a good idea to follow up on tips you get from enthusiastic strangers in pubs. Long story short, you want to nab site 6 or 7, if at all possible. These are set back

Changing leaves make Whispering Falls an especially pretty late-season choice.

KEY INFORMATION

CONTACT: American Land & Leisure for Willamette National Forest, Detroit Ranger District: 541-225-6300, www.fs.usda.gov /recarea/willamette/recarea/?recid=4229

OPEN: Mid-May–mid-September

SITES: 16

WHEELCHAIR ACCESS: Not designated

EACH SITE HAS: Picnic table, fire ring with grill

ASSIGNMENT: First come, first served, or by reservation at 877-444-6777 or recreation.gov

REGISTRATION: Self-registration on-site

AMENITIES: Vault toilets, piped water, garbage service

PARKING: At campsites; $7/additional vehicle

FEE: $16; $10 reservation fee

ELEVATION: 2,000'

RESTRICTIONS:

PETS: On leash only

QUIET HOURS: 10 p.m.–6 a.m.

FIRES: In fire rings only

ALCOHOL: Permitted

OTHER: RVs up to 30'; 14-day stay limit; no chain saws

from the main loop enough to *almost* qualify as walk-in sites, but not far enough to be a pain—and they're surrounded on three sides by thick vegetation, and about as close to the river as you'd want to sleep without risking an unintentional midnight swim. They're also among the farthest sites from the sometimes-busy OR 22, so there's not much, if any, traffic noise. There are really no bad sites here, but these two are just about perfect.

Once you're here, you are well positioned to enjoy any number of outdoor pursuits. Anglers can fish for rainbow trout along the North Santiam, potentially without even having to leave camp. Nearby, Detroit Lake is a busy hub of water-based activity, but it may be too crowded for some, especially in peak summer. For more solitude, head in the other direction and seek out some of the state's best hiking. A rewarding day hike starts from the Marion Forks trailhead, just a few miles down OR 22, up to Marion Lake, passing a few smaller lakes along the way—it's a great goal for a picnic lunch, or you can make it the first leg of a more ambitious backpacking trip, as there are easy connections to the Pacific Crest Trail and other routes from here. (As always, be sure to have a good topo map and compass if you're wandering around out this way.) There's also a fish hatchery at Marion Forks with interesting displays. In operation since 1951, the hatchery raises Chinook salmon and rainbow trout. You can watch the Chinook spawning between late August and into September, and there's a pond at the hatchery where you can watch and feed rainbow trout. And if you're not especially into fish, the surrounding forest is home to deer and elk, as well as eagles, ospreys, grouse, and other local birdlife.

Another excellent nearby hike goes up to the Coffin Mountain Lookout, which provides a view of Mount Jefferson as well as some lovely fields of wildflowers along the way. Not far from here is the Bachelor Mountain trail, where there was a fire lookout until the 1960s. Here you'll be able to appreciate the silver lining of a forest fire: the wide-open slope left in the wake of the fire offers epic views of the Cascades. Both Coffin Mountain and Bachelor trailheads are accessed off of Straight Creek Road (also known as FS 11, also known as Quartzville Scenic Byway), which branches off from OR 22 about 10 miles south of the campground.

For something a little more luxurious, you could make the beautiful drive along FS 46 to Breitenbush, an upscale hot springs retreat where you can have a soak, sauna, yoga class, massage, and meditation session alongside your vegetarian lunch or dinner. (Reservations are required.) Then again, you might be just as happy meditating in your secret hiding spot along the river, back at camp.

Whispering Falls Campground

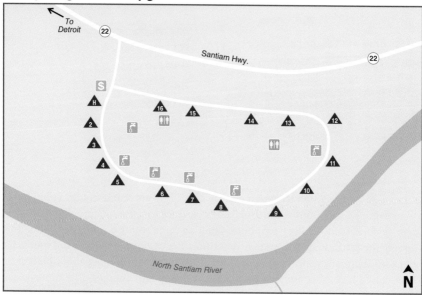

GETTING THERE

From I-5 take Exit 253 in Salem (OR 22 E/OR 99E/Detroit Lake). Head east on OR 22 and drive 57.2 miles (8.3 miles past Detroit); the campground is on the right.

GPS COORDINATES: N44° 41.298'   W122° 00.621'

CENTRAL CASCADES

The Deschutes River winds through Tumalo State Park (see page 94).

17

Cascadia State Park Campground

Beauty ★★★★ Privacy ★★★ Spaciousness ★★★ Quiet ★★★★ Security ★★★★ Cleanliness ★★★★★

Most people speed right on past this little cove of peace and tranquility.

Driving east on US 20 out of Sweet Home, you first pass Foster Lake, a large and decidedly unscenic reservoir created by the U.S. Army Corps of Engineers. Then the road gets a little curvy, the trees get taller and thicker, and you can feel the draw of the high country. You start to speed up, dreaming of what's to come, and . . . what was that? Some kind of a park or something?

Yes, that sign on the left said Cascadia State Park, and it is one of the little-known gems of the Oregon State Park system. It doesn't have the magical attractions of Silver Falls (see page 54) or as much dramatic mountain scenery as Tumalo (see page 94), and the location—so near to the I-5 corridor—might not seem inspiring. But drive down the short access road off US 20 and you'll find yourself in a little cove of peace and tranquility that most people speed right on past.

Cascadia has a manicured feel to it—in a good way, as if somebody designed it to be peaceful and inviting. Turns out, somebody did: The park is a former resort, built to entice visitors to Soda Creek. In the early 20th century, the mineral-filled waters brought enough

Just up US 20, a trailhead leads you to the viewing platform atop Iron Mountain.

KEY INFORMATION

CONTACT: 541-937-1173,
oregonstateparks.org

OPEN: May 1–September 30

SITES: 25

WHEELCHAIR ACCESS: Restrooms, showers

EACH SITE HAS: Picnic table, fire ring

ASSIGNMENT: First come, first served

REGISTRATION: With camp host

AMENITIES: Restrooms, drinking water,
showers, firewood

PARKING: At campsites; $7/additional vehicle

FEE: $17

ELEVATION: 850'

RESTRICTIONS:

PETS: On leash only

QUIET HOURS: 10 p.m.–6 a.m.

FIRES: In fire rings only

ALCOHOL: Permitted

OTHER: RVs and trailers up to 35';
no generators allowed

people here to support a large hotel called the Geisendorfer, which had tennis courts, a garden, and a croquet course. Spend some time in the big mowed meadow by the group camping area, tossing a Frisbee or just soaking up the summer sun, pondering a short saunter down to the river for a swim and some fishing, and you can easily imagine that somebody did a good job putting this place together.

Cascadia spreads out beneath tall firs and hemlocks. In September and October, it's bathed in fall colors from maples, and in spring and summer it's awash in wildflowers. Somehow, even when it's full, the park is nice and quiet. As a camp host once said, "We're just a quiet little family park."

Another comment overheard about Cascadia: "There's nothing there, really, but campsites and forest and some trails and the river." To which we say, exactly! (For the literalists, there are also showers, ADA-accessible restrooms, firewood for sale, drinking water, and recycling facilities—but no RV dump station!)

The South Santiam River is, in these parts, a little wonder of Cascade scenery. It isn't awesome by any means, though in late spring there's often a ton of water in it. By late summer, it's basically a series of deep clear pools surrounded by cliffs and beautiful rock formations, separated by tiny rapids and waterfalls—perfect, in other words, for swimming or skipping around on the rocks, or even some fishing. You'll be lucky to catch anything bigger than 6 inches; the real fishing is below Foster Dam, where overlapping runs of Chinook salmon and steelhead bring folks from all over.

On top of the fishing, swimming, and lounging, Cascadia has two hiking trails that start right in the park: the River Trail runs 1 mile along the South Santiam, with several side trails leading down to the river. The Soda Falls Trail is a bit tougher, gaining 500 feet in less than a mile to 150-foot Lower Soda Creek Falls.

But, as with the fishing, the "real" hiking is not really at Cascadia; it's all over the place, just up US 20. Highlights include two former lookout sites, one atop a huge pillar called Rooster Rock (reached by a steep 2.1-mile trail and some optional rock scrambling) and the other atop Iron Mountain, which you can get to in a steep 1.7 miles or as a 6-mile loop that includes the Cone Peak Trail and a section of the historic Santiam Wagon Road. That last road is of interest in itself; some 20 miles remain of this 19th-century military road, much of which is being developed for multiple users, including "drivers of vintage vehicles and wagons," according to the Willamette National Forest website.

For information on all of these activities and plenty more, stop by the Sweet Home Ranger District (it's right on US 20), visit the website at www.fs.fed.us/r6/willamette, or call the Sweet Home office at 541-367-5168.

Cascadia State Park Campground

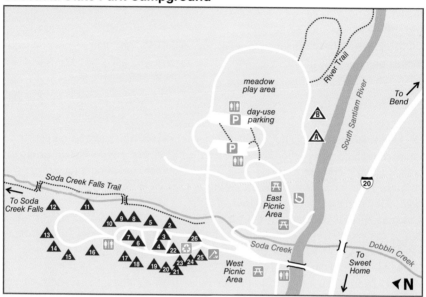

GETTING THERE

From I-5 take Exit 233 (US 20/Albany/Lebanon). Head east on US 20 E and drive 40.2 miles. Turn left onto Dobbin Creek Road and drive across the small bridge ahead; the park entrance will be on your right.

GPS COORDINATES: N44° 23.839'   W122° 28.866'

18

⛺ East Lake Campground

Beauty ★★★★★ Privacy ★★★ Spaciousness ★★★ Quiet ★★★ Security ★★★★★ Cleanliness ★★★★

The Newberry Volcanic National Monument is a wonderland of lava flows, cinder cones, hot springs, obsidian flows, lava caves, forests, and trails.

East Lake is the best of several campgrounds inside the Newberry National Volcanic Monument, and it makes an ideal base for exploring this amazing corner of Oregon. If you've been putting off a visit because of something along the lines of "seen one caldera, seen 'em all," it's time to correct that attitude. Stop whatever you're doing right now and make plans to visit Newberry. It's really amazing. You drive east from US 97, past meadows and trees, ever climbing, and then suddenly you come around a corner and there's this big lake, with forested mountains on the other side. This is Paulina Lake. You keep going for a few more miles, past ever more impressive views, and there's another one! This is East Lake.

Combined, these two lakes cover some 2,300 acres; East Lake averages 65 feet in depth, and Paulina averages 170 with a deepest spot around 250 feet. And both lakes are ringed by trails (13 miles in all) offering access to the shorelines.

There are seven campgrounds within the monument, and in our view, the best are East Lake, Cinder Hill, Little Crater, and Paulina Lake—in that order. We chose to describe East Lake here for a couple of reasons: it's the smallest of the bunch (though still fairly

Many of the campsites have a stunning view of East Lake.
(courtesy of the U.S. Forest Service–Pacific Northwest Region/public domain)

KEY INFORMATION

CONTACT: Hoodoo Recreation Services for Deschutes National Forest, Newberry National Volcanic Monument: 541-383-4000, hoodoorecreation.com, www.fs.usda.gov/recarea/deschutes/recarea/?recid=38346

OPEN: June–mid-October

SITES: 29

WHEELCHAIR ACCESS: Not designated, restroom

EACH SITE HAS: Picnic table, fire ring

ASSIGNMENT: First come, first served, or by reservation at 877-444-6777 or recreation.gov

REGISTRATION: With camp host

AMENITIES: Vault and flush toilets, drinking water, boat launch

PARKING: At campsites; $9/additional vehicle

FEE: $18; $10 reservation fee

ELEVATION: 6,400'

RESTRICTIONS:

PETS: On leash only

QUIET HOURS: 10 p.m.–6 a.m.

FIRES: In fire rings only

ALCOHOL: Permitted

OTHER: RVs and trailers up to 26'

large) and offers the most shade and privacy per site. So start at East Lake, and if it's full, move down the line of campgrounds until you find an open spot. They're all good.

One thing to note, however: This area's charms are not a well-kept secret. The campgrounds can be very busy during summer, especially on weekends. If your schedule allows, try to arrive on a Thursday night to make sure you can snag a spot. East Lake also has a couple of boat launch sites within the campground, which adds to its popularity but also increases the sense of hustle and bustle.

Once you're at the monument, here's something to think about: You're inside the caldera of a volcano, and it's about 4 by 5 miles wide. A caldera is what's left when the summit of a volcano collapses (Crater Lake is another example). In this case, the whole Newberry Volcano is about 20 miles wide. The monument is a wonderland of lava flows, cinder cones, hot springs, obsidian flows, lava caves, forests, and trails.

And fish—really, really big fish. Both lakes are home to rainbow and brown trout, Atlantic salmon, and kokanee. The biggest brown caught there was 22 pounds, 8 ounces; Paulina Lake holds the state record for a brown at 28 pounds, 5 ounces. Ask at the entrance to the monument for the latest restrictions and regulations.

For hiking, there are more than 60 miles of trails to choose from, ranging from short interpretive trails to the 21-mile Crater Rim Trail, which loops around in the high country, exposing you to wide-open views and connections to several other trails, including Paulina Lakeshore (7 miles) and the Paulina Peak Trail.

If you're not up for hiking to Paulina Peak, or can't spare the time, don't worry—you can also drive there. The highest point in the monument (7,984') has a 360-degree view that takes in the caldera and both lakes, the south and west flanks of the volcano, the Cascades, the Fort Rock Basin, and much of Central Oregon. It's said that on a clear day you can see from Mount Adams in Washington to Mount Shasta in California—a spread of some 350 miles. The 4.1-mile Paulina Peak Road is, according to the U.S. Forest Service, steep, dusty, and "quite rough and precipitous in some places." But there's no doubt that it's worth the trip.

One final note to consider for your rapidly upcoming trip to Newberry Monument: It's bear country, as every page on the monument website will remind you. Black bear visits are said to be fairly common in campgrounds, so do your part by following all the food storage regulations.

And don't let the bear thing—or anything else, for that matter—deter you, because you are going to East Lake, and soon. Right?

East Lake Campground

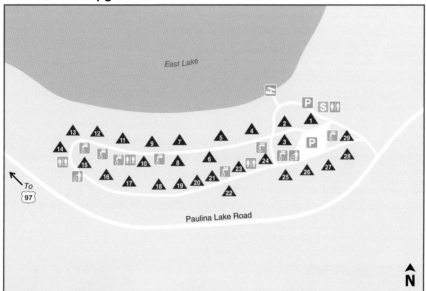

GETTING THERE

From the intersection of US 20 and US 97 in Bend, take US 97 S and drive 24.7 miles, then turn left onto Paulina Lake Road/Forest Service Road 21. Drive 16.6 miles and follow signs for East Lake Campground; the entrance will be on your left.

GPS COORDINATES: N43° 43.055'   W121° 12.575'

19

Frissell Crossing Campground

Beauty ★★★★★ Privacy ★★★★ Spaciousness ★★★★ Quiet ★★★★★ Security ★★ Cleanliness ★★★

During the week, you may have the place almost to yourself.

It's cliché to say that getting somewhere is half the fun, but with Frissell Crossing it's true. The campground sits along the Aufderheide Memorial Drive—one of the first 50 drives in the country to receive federal scenic byway designation in 1988, it's named for a former Willamette National Forest supervisor. The road is legendary among those who know about it. Part of the West Cascades Scenic Byway, it's a delightfully twisty stretch of pavement between Westfir and Rainbow and a favorite among motorcyclists, along with, well, anybody who likes the idea of a scenic drive to and from the middle of nowhere.

It's easy to let your imagination run wild as you wind along the Aufderheide, whether you approach it from the South Fork McKenzie River side on the north or from the North Fork Middle Fork Willamette on the south. Some of you will read that sentence at least twice, puzzling over the route. The road, 65 miles long, follows in modern style the pioneering wagon route established by miners and loggers in the late 1800s. As it rises and falls through dense old-growth forest and passes over a low-elevation saddle between the two river drainages, it reveals a rich mosaic of historical, geological, and cultural significance. It would be easy to fill a week absorbing it all, between backcountry exploration and roadside edification.

The Landis cabin marks the highest point on the Aufderheide Memorial Drive.
(photographed by Martin Bravenboer/Flickr/CC BY 2.0 [creativecommons.org/licenses/by/2.0])

KEY INFORMATION

CONTACT: American Land & Leisure for Willamette National Forest, McKenzie River Ranger District: 541-822-3381, www.fs.usda.gov/recarea/willamette /recarea/?recid=4368

OPEN: Early May–mid-September

SITES: 12

WHEELCHAIR ACCESS: Not designated

EACH SITE HAS: Picnic table, fire ring with grill

ASSIGNMENT: First come, first served

REGISTRATION: Self-registration on-site

AMENITIES: Vault toilets, hand-pumped water

PARKING: At campsites; $7/additional vehicle

FEE: $14

ELEVATION: 2,600'

RESTRICTIONS:

PETS: On leash only

QUIET HOURS: 10 p.m.–6 a.m.

FIRES: In fire rings only

ALCOHOL: Permitted

OTHER: RVs up to 36' (turnaround space is limited); no hookups; 14-day stay limit; no chain saws

If you don't have that kind of time but still want to get the most of what the Aufderheide has to offer, take along an audio guide. The U.S. Forest Service provides, free of charge, a CD that you can pick up and drop off at the Middle Fork Ranger District and/ or the McKenzie River Ranger District offices. This is a far better idea than having your nose buried in a guidebook (excluding this volume, of course). For one thing, it's kind of dangerous to read and drive at the same time—audio guides are definitely the way to go. With any luck, the idea might signal a trend for other agencies, which could benefit from marketing their scenic byways in a similar fashion.

Frissell Crossing Campground sits about one-third of the way down the Aufderheide road from its northern terminus, along the South Fork McKenzie River, which at this point has made a quick descent from its source in the Mink Lake Basin. Although you'll pass several other very appealing campgrounds along the route, Frissell Crossing has one thing most others don't: piped water. The camping sites are situated well away from the main road too, which is always best.

Minimally developed sites are spread around an open meadow, retaining in ambience the true essence of the Aufderheide and the primarily roadless wilderness land surrounding the campground. A high canopy of old-growth Douglas fir further lends to the sense of space at Frissell Crossing, while generous low-growing vegetation creates a gentle buffer between campsites and adds just the right measure of privacy without claustrophobia. The McKenzie River passes through grassy, rhododendron-shrouded banks on the campground's southern border.

With only 12 sites, it's unlikely you'll ever feel crowded, but sites 6 and 7 on the eastern edge of the campground loop are the most removed from the main activity area. During the week, even in peak summer season, you may have the place almost to yourself. There's certainly no guarantee, but the Aufderheide isn't exactly a direct or convenient route to anywhere in particular and is not among the more heavily traveled back roads in Oregon.

Frissell Crossing makes an excellent base camp for hiking forays into a multitude of nearby wilderness areas. Due east is the south-central sector of the Three Sisters Wilderness, which laps over into the Western Cascades and is far less traveled than its northern counterpart. This region of the wilderness is home to a stunning cluster of alpine lakes and the headwaters of the South Fork McKenzie. On Frissell's north side is the French Pete Creek area, the inclusion of which into Three Sisters Wilderness in 1978 preserved some of the most accessible examples of ancient low-elevation old growth. A short drive south of Frissell is the trailhead for access into the northern portion of the Waldo Lake Wilderness.

Driving the Aufderheide requires that you check the gas gauge first. There are absolutely no services along the route, and side trips can eat up your fuel supply. Bring plenty of food rations too. You just never know where the Willamette's version of the Yellow Brick Road may lead. Ruby hiking boots, anyone?

Frissell Crossing Campground

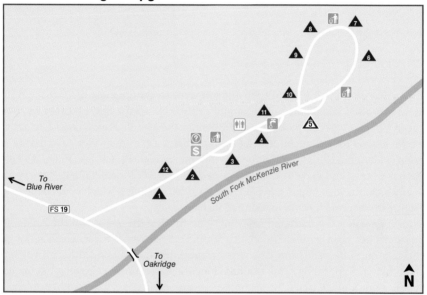

GETTING THERE

From I-5 take Exit 194A in Eugene to head east on OR 126. In 6.4 miles turn left to remain on OR 126, and go another 38.9 miles. Turn right onto Cougar Dam Road/Forest Service Road 19 and drive 0.4 mile. Turn right onto FS 19/Aufderheide Memorial Drive and drive 21 miles to Frissell Crossing Campground. The campground entrance is on the left.

From the intersection of US 20 and US 97 in Bend, head west on US 20 for 47.7 miles. Turn left onto OR 126 E, and drive 29.3 miles. Turn left onto Cougar Dam Road/FS 19 and drive 0.4 mile. Turn right onto FS 19/Aufderheide Memorial Drive and drive 21 miles to Frissell Crossing Campground. The campground entrance is on the left.

GPS COORDINATES: N43° 57.451'   W122° 05.156'

Islet Campground

Beauty ★★★★★ Privacy ★★★ Spaciousness ★★★ Quiet ★★★ Security ★★★★ Cleanliness ★★★★★

The lake itself offers wondrous paddling and sailing opportunities, including to some 50 primitive campsites around the lake.

Though not many people seem to know about it, Waldo Lake is Oregon's second-biggest natural lake (after Crater Lake), with a surface area of 9.8 square miles. It is also Oregon's second-deepest natural lake (again, after Crater Lake), averaging 128 feet with a maximum depth of 420 feet. It is reputed to be one of the purest lakes on Earth, some say nearly as pure as distilled water, because the only sources of water coming into the lake are precipitation and snowmelt. Partly because of the lake's purity, when the weather is calm you can see 120 feet down into it. It is also ringed by old-growth forest and wilderness, with mountain views, trails all over the place, practically no motorboats allowed, and several great campsites.

The three campgrounds around the lake (Islet, North Waldo, and Shadow Bay) are pretty much the same, but Islet is the smallest one, so we're recommending it. All three have the same facilities, basic layouts, and ideal locations right on the shore of the lake, so in the grand scheme of things, it doesn't matter where you camp, just as long as you're at Waldo Lake.

And here's why: The lake itself offers wondrous paddling and sailing opportunities, including to some 50 primitive campsites around the lake. You can also paddle out to Rhododendron Island, which, as the name suggests, is covered with rhododendrons, in full bloom

Morning fog rolls across Waldo Lake.

KEY INFORMATION

CONTACT: American Land & Leisure for Willamette National Forest, Middle Fork Ranger District: 541-782-2283, www.fs.usda.gov/recarea/willamette /recreation/recarea/?recid=4501

OPEN: Late June–October, depending on snow levels

SITES: 55

WHEELCHAIR ACCESS: Restrooms

EACH SITE HAS: Picnic table, fire ring

ASSIGNMENT: First come, first served

REGISTRATION: With camp host

AMENITIES: Composting and vault toilets, piped drinking water, garbage service, recycle center, boat launch, interpretive sign

PARKING: At campsites and in boat-launch area; $7/additional vehicle

FEE: $22

ELEVATION: 5,400'

RESTRICTIONS:
PETS: On leash only

QUIET HOURS: 10 p.m.–6 a.m.

FIRES: In fire rings only

ALCOHOL: Permitted

OTHER: RVs and trailers up to 24'; 14-day stay limit; no chain saws; motorized boats that travel under 10 mph only

---

starting usually around mid-June. The island is about 1.5 miles northeast of the ramp in Shadow Bay Campground. Note that camping is not allowed on Rhododendron Island itself.

(Unfortunately, the mosquitoes that live at Waldo Lake also thrive in early summer—they can be especially brutal mid-June–August, so come prepared with your favorite pest defense.)

The only motorized boats allowed on the lake are those that travel at less than 10 miles per hour—which means that it stays pretty quiet out there. Even die-hard anglers tend not to swarm Waldo Lake, as there aren't all that many fish to be had. This place is all about quiet exploration, contemplative paddling, and then relaxing at a comfy lakeside campsite.

And then there's the hiking, starting with the Jim Weaver Loop Trail. Also known as the Waldo Lake Trail, it was renamed and made a National Recreation Trail in 2008. The easy trail follows the shoreline for 22 miles, in the process passing through all the campgrounds and connecting with about a dozen other trails. Some of these trails, west of the lake, lead into the Waldo Lake Wilderness, where you'll find 84 more miles of trails and 37,162 lake-filled acres. (Jim Weaver, in case you're wondering, was an Oregon Democrat who served in the state legislature 1975–1987 and was an outspoken advocate for natural-resource conservation projects, including the designation of new wilderness areas north of Waldo Lake in the 1980s.)

North of the lake is another trail area with more than a half dozen other trails, many leading north toward the Taylor Burn Trail Area and, eventually, the southern part of the Three Sisters Wilderness. Passing through all of this, just east of Waldo Lake, is the beloved Pacific Crest Trail, which crosses the Willamette National Forest for 118 miles. A favorite spot on that trail, and a recommended destination for a day hike from the campground, is Charlton Lake, which is just off a road east of Waldo Lake. Other worthy goals include Twins Peak (3.3 miles), Maiden Peak (10.4 miles), and Waldo Mountain Lookout at 6,357 feet. You can hike to the lookout and back in a day from North Waldo Campground, but the U.S. Forest Service is particularly insistent that you get good trail maps and know what you're up to. The website warns that the trip "requires several judgment turns and some rather extreme changes in direction. It can be very confusing."

The only other confusing thing around here is the question of why there are still campers in Oregon who haven't been to Waldo Lake.

Islet Campground

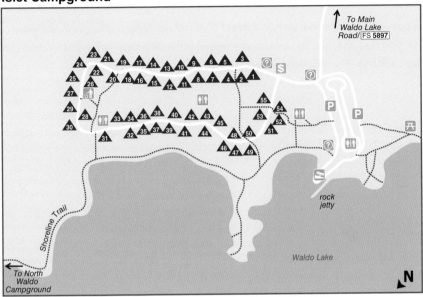

GETTING THERE

From the intersection of US 20 and US 97 in Bend, take US 97 S for 56.3 miles, and take the exit for OR 58 W/Oakridge/Eugene. On OR 58 W, drive 27.1 miles. Turn right onto Waldo Lake Road/Forest Service Road 5897 and drive 11 miles. Turn left to remain on FS 5897, and go another 1.3 miles. Turn left, and go 0.5 mile. Turn left onto FS 5898 and drive 1.2 miles to the campground.

GPS COORDINATES: N43° 44.877' W122° 00.447'

21

Mallard Marsh Campground

Beauty ★★★★★ Privacy ★★★★★ Spaciousness ★★★★★ Quiet ★★★★★ Security ★★★★
Cleanliness ★★★★★

The combination of Hosmer Lake's deepest blue waters, azure skies, brilliant green marsh grasses, and colorful waterfowl—topped off with a snow-streaked volcano cone as the backdrop—is undeniably exquisite.

For reasons unknown, Mallard Marsh gets short shrift in much of the literature about the Central Oregon Cascade Lakes region. Perhaps because the campground name doesn't reflect its location on Hosmer Lake? Perhaps because the word *marsh* implies a soggy, bug-infested ordeal? Or maybe just because there are so many great camping options in this Mecca for outdoor adventure?

Whatever the reason, we'd like to raise awareness by saying that Mallard Marsh is probably one of the prettiest campground settings you'll find listed in this book. It has lots of competition from countless other lakeside camping areas in the region, but none of the others quite measure up to the outstanding tent camping features of Mallard Marsh. That's saying a lot, but the combination of Hosmer Lake's deepest blue waters, azure skies, brilliant green marsh grasses, and colorful waterfowl—topped off with a snow-streaked volcano cone as the backdrop—is undeniably exquisite. It simply doesn't get much more picturesque!

The campground itself maintains a very natural countenance to further add to its charm. Driving in past the busy boat launch, you can pick your spot as you pass between the sites,

Mount Bachelor as seen from Hosmer Lake

KEY INFORMATION

CONTACT: Hoodoo Recreation for Deschutes National Forest, Bend–Fort Rock Ranger District: 541-338-7869, hoodoorecreation .com, www.fs.usda.gov/recarea/deschutes /recarea/?recid=38920

OPEN: Mid-June–late September, depending on snow levels

SITES: 14

WHEELCHAIR ACCESS: Not designated

EACH SITE HAS: Picnic table, fire ring

ASSIGNMENT: First come, first served

REGISTRATION: Self-registration on-site

AMENITIES: Vault toilets, no piped water, boat launch nearby

PARKING: At campsites; $5/additional vehicle

FEE: $10

ELEVATION: 5,000'

RESTRICTIONS:

PETS: On leash only

QUIET HOURS: 10 p.m.–6 a.m.

FIRES: In fire rings only

ALCOHOL: Permitted

OTHER: RVs up to 22'; no hookups; electric boat motors only

roughly half on the lakeside and the others discreetly tucked away on little knolls or in slight depressions. All of the sites are situated under tall stands of lodgepole pine, Douglas fir, and mountain hemlock, with heavy undergrowth of salal, laurel, and huckleberry providing effective natural screening for privacy. The sites along the lake tend to be a bit more open and enjoy the morning sun's rays earlier. The sites that are set farther back receive filtered sunlight all day long and probably are less mosquito-prone.

In general, the spaciousness of the sites and the generous greenbelts between them lend a delightfully uncrowded feel to the camping experience at Mallard Marsh, even at the height of a busy summer week.

In this setting, Hosmer Lake is a sport angler's dream, but it's one that comes with a few regulations. In order to challenge the wily Atlantic salmon and brown trout that ply the lake's waters, only fly-fishing with barbless hooks is allowed. Nonmotorized boats are the approved mode of travel.

While sailboaters and windsurfers head for Elk Lake when the wind is up, Hosmer is ideal for muscle-powered water travel (for example, kayaks and canoes); these are much better suited to the quiet ambience of the place anyway. Encompassing only 160 acres, Hosmer makes it easy to spend a lazy afternoon exploring the bordering wetlands and taking in a little bird-watching. Don't forget the binoculars.

Should the trail call you out of your lakeside comfort, the Cascade Lakes region is home to many high-country rambles. From the Cascade Lakes Highway, you can satisfy your explorer's urge with trailheads in all directions. Quite possibly, you'll be following along routes established by the early trappers and adventurers who left their indelible historical mark on the region. You could easily spend a full week just on the trails of the Three Sisters Wilderness (due west of Hosmer Lake), discovering one alpine lake gem after another and getting your boots dusty on a section of the Pacific Crest Trail in one of its easiest wilderness access points. From some of the higher vantage points, you can practically watch the weather patterns changing overhead, as this is a meeting point for air currents where rapid climatic transition occurs.

Like many of the ancient landmarks that give Oregon its remarkable diversity, the Cascade Lakes region was defined geologically by cataclysmic events that occurred millions of years ago. Unlike many other parts of Oregon, the contours of the landscape, the composition of the soils, and the nature of the vegetation make it possible to view many of Central Oregon's treasures up close. A good place to start is the Lava Lands Visitor Center or the excellent and fascinating High Desert Museum in Bend. Spend an afternoon there and you'll leave with a new, better-informed appreciation for the natural wonders that characterize this region.

One word of warning if you intend to do some day-tripping: The closest services to Mallard Marsh are either in Bend or La Pine, and it is easy to lose track of time and distance out here. Make sure you've got a full gas tank.

Mallard Marsh Campground

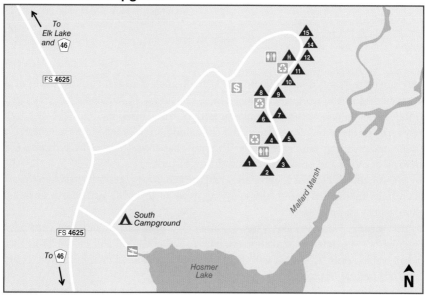

GETTING THERE

From the intersection of US 20 and US 97 in Bend, take US 97 S to Exit 139. Head west on SW Reed Market Road, going through several traffic circles, for 1.4 miles. At the traffic circle, take the third exit (left) onto Cascade Lakes National Scenic Byway/SW Century Drive for 32.6 miles. Turn left onto Forest Service Road 4625 and drive 1.3 miles. At the Y, turn right down the gravel road. You'll pass South Campground on the right side, then Mallard Marsh.

GPS COORDINATES: N43° 57.801'   W121° 47.140'

22

Paradise Campground

Beauty ★★★★★ Privacy ★★★★ Spaciousness ★★★★ Quiet ★★★★ Security ★★★ Cleanliness ★★★★

Camp beside the mighty McKenzie River, surrounded by old-growth Douglas fir and cedar trees strung with thick green moss.

A quintessential Oregon riverside campground, the aptly named Paradise was built in the 1930s by the Civilian Conservation Corps—as were many of the nicest and most durable recreational facilities in the state. It's the kind of place you see once and dream about for years: a string of perfectly laid-out campsites pocketed away beside the mighty McKenzie River, surrounded by old-growth Douglas fir and cedar trees strung with thick green moss. This is Oregon tent camping at its finest . . . which, sadly, means it can often be tough to snag a spot here. Luckily, there are several other campgrounds along this road, many of them almost as nice—but this is our favorite. For the best chances of getting a spot, as well as the opportunity to be completely surrounded by intense fall colors, visit Paradise at the tail end of the season, just before it closes for the winter.

In terms of selecting your campsite, you can't really go wrong here: Some of them back onto the river, and the rest are nestled into the woods. There's enough space and enough ground cover between each site to ensure privacy, despite the fairly large size of the campground. But if you do want to hang out with your neighbors, there are plenty of activities that

Aptly named Paradise Campground is set amid a storybook forest.

KEY INFORMATION

CONTACT: American Land & Leisure for Willamette National Forest, McKenzie River Ranger District: 801-226-3564, www.fs .usda.gov/recarea/willamette /recarea/?recid=4380

OPEN: Early May–mid-October

SITES: 61

WHEELCHAIR ACCESS: Restrooms, day-use area

EACH SITE HAS: Picnic table, fire ring with grill

ASSIGNMENT: First come, first served, or by reservation at 877-444-6777 or recreation.gov

REGISTRATION: Self-registration on-site

AMENITIES: Flush toilets, piped water, amphitheater, day-use picnic area

PARKING: At campsites; $7/additional vehicle

FEE: $22; $10 reservation fee

ELEVATION: 1,600'

RESTRICTIONS:

PETS: On leash only

QUIET HOURS: None specified

FIRES: In fire rings only

ALCOHOL: Permitted

OTHER: Trailers up to 40'; no hookups; 14-day stay limit; no chain saws

would provide a chance to do so. Parents and curious campers will be happy to know that the campground has an amphitheater (which, like the picnic grounds, is wheelchair accessible), where rangers lead educational programs during the peak summer season. And the day-use picnic area offers opportunities to fish the river. But you can also arrange for more ambitious fishing expeditions, as well as a host of other activities that can be pursued along the 90-mile corridor of the McKenzie River.

Maybe the best-known of these is the McKenzie River National Recreation Trail, a 25-mile singletrack mountain bike and hiking path that starts in a lava field north of Clear Lake, passes by several other lakes, pools, hot springs, and waterfalls, and slowly makes its way alongside the path of the river. Many mountain bikers say it's some of the best single-track riding in the state. The lower half is a little easier, if you have kids or newbies in your crew. It's also a popular area for trail running. To reach the trailhead, take OR 126 to the north side of Clear Lake Resort, then turn right onto Forest Service Road 777 and follow signs to the Upper McKenzie River Trailhead at road's end. You can also pick up the trail right there at Paradise Campground, which is near the trail's southern terminus, and follow it in either direction, depending on how much time and energy you have. A number of side trails branch off the main path, making for some excellent day-hiking opportunities if you have a decent map.

One appealing option: Just over 10 miles up the road (OR 126), also reachable by hiking the McKenzie River National Recreation Trail northeast from Paradise Campground, is Tamolitch Falls, also known as the Blue Pool. It's a fascinating phenomenon: Some 1,600 years ago, lava buried a stretch of the river, and the pool at the base of the Tamolitch Falls is where it resurfaces. The falls are dry most of the year, apart from especially rainy periods. The turquoise pool might look tempting on a hot day, but be careful: You're allowed to jump in, but the water temperature averages 37°, meaning that if you linger, you'll risk hypothermia (even in summer).

Just a 3-minute drive east along OR 126, you'll come across Belknap Hot Springs, a charmingly rustic wilderness resort with two hot-springs mineral pools, soaking tubs, cabins, RV sites and camping, a café, a lodge, and a whimsical outdoor sculpture garden. The place has been open to the public since the 1870s, and some of the facilities might be a little rough around the edges, but it's a great way to reward yourself with a soak after a long day of hiking.

Parts of the river are also popular for rafting and kayaking. The possibilities range from placid drifting to Classes I–V whitewater rapids, depending on where you go. The northernmost section, near Sahalie Falls, is the most challenging and has a mandatory exit by the falls. There are more than 30 boat ramps along the river, so grab a map, have a chat with the rangers at the office, and get going!

Paradise Campground

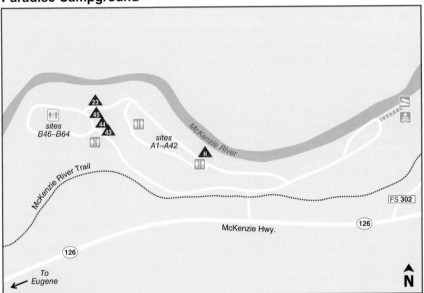

GETTING THERE

From the intersection of US 20 and US 97 in Bend, head west on US 20 for 47.7 miles. Turn left onto OR 126 E. Drive 20.6 miles and the campground entrance will be on your right.

From I-5 take Exit 194A in Eugene and head east on OR 126. In 47.6 miles the campground will be on your left (about 3.8 miles past McKenzie Bridge).

GPS COORDINATES: N44° 11.042'   W122° 05.408'

23

Riverside Campground

Beauty ★★★★★ Privacy ★★★ Spaciousness ★★★★ Quiet ★★★★ Security ★★★ Cleanliness ★★

This is one of many campgrounds near the anglers' paradise that is the Metolius River.

Oh, the magical and mysterious Metolius. It wells up clear and bright from an underground spring at the base of Black Butte and provides one of the finest trout habitats around (catch-and-release fly-fishing only) before emptying into the Deschutes River.

There are varying theories about the exact origins of this headwater phenomenon, but the prevailing one seems to be that ancient earth movements blocked the original Metolius and forced it to find an alternate route. It took a while, but it eventually found an outlet at the base of Black Butte. Today, it bubbles and burbles at a rate of 50,000 gallons per minute (right before your very eyes!) to create one of the coldest and clearest rivers in Oregon.

That's why trout like it so much. However, there was a time when salmon sought its cooling waters too. The name *Metolius* derives from *mptolyas*, a term that showed up in a 19th-century Pacific Railroad survey report. The reference is to a variety of salmon that is no longer found in the river. These days, conservation groups are working to restore native salmon (Chinook and sockeye) to the river, but it's slow going. Anglers, on the other hand, will be in plentiful supply if you come to the Metolius at the height of the fly-fishing season.

The number of campgrounds on or near the Metolius is staggering, and they are there primarily to serve the abundance of anglers. In addition to Riverside, campers can choose from Camp Sherman, Allingham, Smiling River, Pine Rest (our next choice if Riverside is full), Gorge, Allen Springs, Pioneer Ford, and Lower Bridge, strung along the river at intervals.

The mighty Metolius River, as seen from walk-in-only Riverside Campground near the river's head

KEY INFORMATION

CONTACT: Hoodoo Recreation Services for Deschutes National Forest, Detroit Ranger District: 541-338-7869, hoodoorecreation .com, www.fs.usda.gov/recarea/willamette /recreation/camping-cabins /recarea/?recid=4224

OPEN: May–early October

SITES: 16

WHEELCHAIR ACCESS: Not designated

EACH SITE HAS: Picnic table, fire ring with grill

ASSIGNMENT: First come, first served

REGISTRATION: Self-registration on-site

AMENITIES: Vault toilets, hand-pumped water

PARKING: At access road, roughly 200–400 yards from campground; $7/additional vehicle

FEE: $14

ELEVATION: 3,000'

RESTRICTIONS:

PETS: On leash only

QUIET HOURS: 10 p.m.–6 a.m.

FIRES: In fire rings only

ALCOHOL: Permitted

OTHER: RVs up to 21'; no hookups; 14-day stay limit

Riverside is notable in that it has only walk-in sites, which are spacious, grassy, and well situated under stands of majestic old ponderosa pine. (Despite the name, though, only a couple of the sites, 13 and 16, sit right along the bank of the river.) Parking spaces are numbered to correspond with campsites, each within a reasonable distance of the other, but the best sites (those closest to the river) might suddenly seem a long way away if you've got a lot of heavy, cumbersome gear. A small wheelbarrow would be quite useful.

This area of Central Oregon is characterized by warm—even hot—and dry summers and cold, snowy winters. Upland areas have been known to receive as much as 20 feet of snow, and many trails will be blocked well into May. The terrain is laid with a volcanic base, out of which spills a dazzling collage of crystalline streams, creeks, and rivers. Dotting the landscape are ancient lava flows, dormant and deteriorated craters, sparkling inlays of obsidian, rugged basalt cliffs, flat-topped mesas and buttes, and numerous lakes.

Dominating the landscape in various stages of geologic splendor are the snowcapped peaks to the west. In order from north to south, they are Mount Jefferson, Mount Washington, North Sister, Middle Sister, South Sister, and, last but not least, despite its forlorn name, Broken Top.

Hiking is one of the best ways to fully appreciate the diversity of this region. There are actually four distinct geographic zones, all observable at once: the high-alpine slopes of the volcanoes, with meadows of wildflowers and crumbling lava rock; subalpine forests of ponderosa pine and mountain hemlock nourished by cascading streams and glacial lakes; steep-walled canyons that protect the last of the old-growth fir; and arid pockets of lodgepole pine interspersed with bear grass.

Besides foot travel, other ways to take in the scenery are on horseback and mountain bike. Retrace the routes of such early-day explorers as Lewis and Clark, Kit Carson, and John Fremont on the Metolius-Windigo Trail. Outfitters in Sisters can help you with any hoofed mode of travel.

For cyclists, a 30-mile loop trip along the crest of Green Ridge provides panoramic views of the Cascades. It's a climb of 1,700 feet to the top, and it's highly recommended to have a map of the route and surrounding trails handy as you ride. In fact, this is good advice for anyone who plans to explore places not in the immediate vicinity of Forest Service Road 14 along the Metolius. There is a crazy network of spur roads that can easily lead you astray if you don't know your way around.

Be aware that the opposite side of the Metolius at Riverside is private land and should be respected as such—important to keep in mind if you're planning to do any paddling along the river. It's 28.5 miles from the campground to Lake Billy Chinook, a section rated as Class III–IV whitewater rapids. (It's worth checking with rangers before you set out, as reports indicate that the river is often clogged with enough debris to make passage difficult. Luckily, there are plenty of other great paddling options in the vicinity.)

Other highlights of a stay at Riverside Campground include short walks to Metolius Spring and Jack Creek Spring, the Metolius River Canyon near Camp Sherman, and the Wizard Falls Fish Hatchery (a surprisingly beautiful setting, unlike most hatcheries).

Riverside Campground

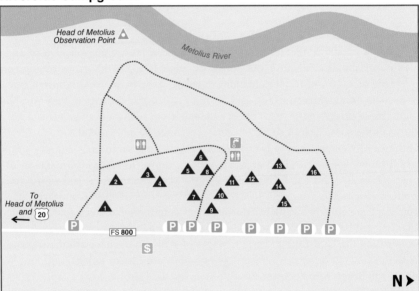

GETTING THERE

From the intersection of US 20 and US 97 in Bend, head west on US 20 for 28.4 miles. Or from I-5 take Exit 233 in Albany and head east on US 20 for 89.6 miles. Turn north onto Forest Service Road 14/Camp Sherman Road (a left from eastbound, a right from westbound). Drive 4.8 miles, around the base of Black Butte, to the campground on the left. Camp Sherman offers some services.

GPS COORDINATES: N44° 26.458'   W121° 38.107'

24

⚠ Rujada Campground

Beauty ★★★★ Privacy ★★★★★ Spaciousness ★★★★ Quiet ★★★★ Security ★★★★ Cleanliness ★★★★

Rujada is located in the upper reaches of the Umpqua National Forest, a sprawling 1 million acres on the western slopes of the Cascades.

Much as we might like to daydream, not every camping adventure can be a weeklong planning and preparation extravaganza. Sometimes you just want a spot that doesn't require all your wayfinding skills and a full tank of gas to reach, but still gives you the experience of having escaped to the woods. If you've only got a night or two to spare, welcome to Rujada, a campground that seems much farther from civilization than it actually is. (If you want to make it seem like a longer trip, head out there on your bicycle.)

A mere 22 miles east of Cottage Grove up the Row River Road (which turns into FS 17), Rujada sits alone in creekside luxury at the base of Rose Hill. Rujada is located in the upper reaches of the Umpqua National Forest, a sprawling 1 million acres on the western slopes of the Cascades. The forest is characterized by the striking contrasts between waterfalls, whitewater-river canyons, mountaintop vistas, and the ever-present green, green, green of ancient forests with shaggy coats of moss and lichen.

Currin Bridge, built in 1925, is one of many historic covered bridges near Rujada Campground.

KEY INFORMATION

CONTACT: Umpqua National Forest, Cottage Grove Ranger District: 541-767-5000, www.fs.usda.gov/recarea/umpqua/recarea/?recid=63436

OPEN: Late May–September

SITES: 15

WHEELCHAIR ACCESS: Restrooms, site 15

EACH SITE HAS: Picnic table, fire ring with grill

ASSIGNMENT: First come, first served, or 8 sites by reservation at 877-444-6777 or recreation.gov

REGISTRATION: Self-registration on-site

AMENITIES: Flush toilets, piped water, garbage service, large day-use picnic areas, horseshoes, play equipment, swimming, camp host in high season

PARKING: At campsites; $5/additional vehicle

FEE: $12

ELEVATION: 1,200'

RESTRICTIONS:

PETS: On leash only

QUIET HOURS: 10 p.m.–6 a.m.

FIRES: In fire rings only

ALCOHOL: Permitted

OTHER: RVs up to 22'; no hookups; 14-day stay limit; no fireworks

Rujada Campground is a microcosm of the Umpqua's ecosystems, with the clear and refreshing waters of Layng Creek at its feet, an expansive understory of ferns skirting its boundaries, stands of second-growth Douglas fir scattered throughout, and three dramatic waterfalls a short distance up FS 17: Moon Falls, Spirit Falls, and Pinard Falls.

The campground is laid out in classic, circular fashion, as was the trend when the Civilian Conservation Corps first developed campgrounds, including this one, back in the 1930s. You can see evidence of its early origins at the historic registration booth in the picnic area.

Most of Rujada's 15 sites are tucked deep into vegetated pockets, affording the ultimate in privacy. Site 4 is the closest in proximity to a delightfully secluded swimming hole on Layng Creek that attracts day users as well as campers. (If you can't find it, ask a camp host where it is; there's nothing at the campground pointing it out, and dense underbrush keeps it hidden.) Each campsite has plenty of space for a large tent and is appointed with a concrete fire ring with grate and a standard but sturdy wooden picnic table with the well-worn look of camping days gone by.

Rujada is not the kind of campground that inspires robust activity. Rather, it's a place of relaxation and serenity with perhaps a smattering of youthful vigor in the adjoining playing field, where the kids can romp around on well-maintained playground equipment. If you're looking for a way to stretch your legs, consider hiking the Swordfern Trail, an easy walk of just over a mile that follows Layng Creek partway, overtakes an old abandoned logging road, and completes its loop near the picnic area. For another diversion in the immediate vicinity, the three waterfalls farther up FS 17 are must-sees and require little effort to reach. Catch Spirit Falls in early afternoon for the best photographic light, as it stays shrouded in shadows most of the day. Moon Falls is best viewed during periods of late spring or early summer runoff, when the 125-foot plummet is at full tilt. If a scenic drive is on the agenda, you're in luck: this area is rich with historic covered bridges, including Mosby Creek Bridge, the oldest in Lane County, built in 1920; and the red-and-white Currin Bridge, where Row River meets Layng Road.

If this isn't enough to fill up your weekend, a drive up to Fairview Lookout and Musick Guard Station offers superb views and a taste of history. On the clearest of days, you can see both Mount Hood to the north and Mount Shasta to the south in California. The guard station has been placed on the National Register of Historic Places, and the lookout (rebuilt in 1972) has served as a radar receptor in the past and is still used as a fire lookout during the peak of fire season (August and September). Both the cabin and lookout tower are available to rent. Pick up brochures for both facilities at the Cottage Grove Ranger District office.

If you have time left over after these excursions, you may want to take the high-road route up and over Patterson Mountain, which drops down into the Oakridge area. FS 17 switches to FS 5840 as it passes from Umpqua to Willamette National Forest. It's a little-known backcountry drive that you can easily fit into a loose itinerary, and that may inspire you to return for another weekend.

Rujada Campground

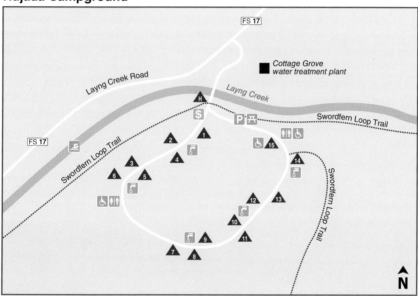

GETTING THERE

From I-5 S, take Exit 174 in Cottage Grove, turn left (east) onto Row River Road, and go 18.4 miles to Forest Service Road 17/Layng Creek Road. Drive 2 miles to the campground entrance on the right. Cross Layng Creek and you're there.

GPS COORDINATES: N43° 42.433'   W122° 44.550'

25

Scott Lake Campground

Beauty ★★★★★ Privacy ★★★★★ Spaciousness ★★★★★ Quiet ★★★★★ Security ★★★★ Cleanliness ★★★

For peace, quiet, and scenery in tent camping, Scott Lake is the best place to be if you're exploring Mount Washington and Three Sisters.

No matter how many times you go camping in Oregon, chances are, at some point, you'll arrive in a place of such natural beauty, such peace and tranquility, that you can't believe you've never been here before—or that it's so devoid of people. It's especially likely that you'll have one of those moments the first time you visit Scott Lake.

There are three obvious reasons so few people camp at Scott Lake, and two of them will work to your advantage. One is that it is almost completely without services: no drinking water, no cut firewood, relatively bare-bones campsites. Another is that all the sites are walk-in, which means no RVs and probably not too many portable stereos.

If you want to know the third reason so few people go there, visit in July and check out the mosquito population. The mosquitoes at Scott Lake in July inspire fear and dread among even the hardiest park rangers. So put this one down for mid-August, at least—which has an added advantage, because that's when the flowers in the nearby wilderness areas will be blooming.

A rough guess is that Scott Lake Campground is, as the crow flies, 1 mile from the Mount Washington Wilderness (52,000+ acres, 28 lakes, one volcano at 7,794') and 0.5 mile from the Three Sisters Wilderness (242,000+ acres, 260 miles of trails, countless lakes, three volcanoes over 10,000').

Spend a tranquil day canoeing Scott Lake.

KEY INFORMATION

CONTACT: Willamette National Forest, McKenzie River Ranger District: 541-822-3381, www.fs.usda.gov/recarea/willamette/recarea/?recid=4382

OPEN: Mid-June–late October, depending on OR 242 status

SITES: 18 walk-in

WHEELCHAIR ACCESS: Restrooms

EACH SITE HAS: Fire ring

ASSIGNMENT: First come, first served

REGISTRATION: Self-registration on-site

AMENITIES: Vault toilet, no drinking water

PARKING: Along the road, up to 200 yards from sites

FEE: $5; Northwest Forest Pass or other interagency pass would suffice

ELEVATION: 4,800'

RESTRICTIONS:

PETS: On leash only

QUIET HOURS: None specified

FIRES: In fire rings only

ALCOHOL: Permitted

OTHER: No trailers; 14-day stay limit; no chain saws

We could fill a book about the beauty of these two areas—in fact, it's been done, several times over. What we want to convey is this: for the person who seeks peace, quiet, and scenery in tent camping, Scott Lake is the best place to be if you're exploring Mount Washington and Three Sisters. With tent-only sites scattered around the shore of broad, shallow Scott Lake, and others in the trees, you are almost guaranteed to have some space all to yourself. Scott Lake is actually shaped kind of like a big number 3, with sites dotting the left side of the lake. So from the parking area at the Benson Trail trailhead, which is as far north as you can drive, you can walk straight toward the visible water to look for sites, or you can follow the wide trail north to others at the midsection of the 3, or you can go even farther along the trail and look for more spots farther up.

The views from the lowest section are the best; you'll be looking right across the lake at the Three Sisters. The lake isn't much for fishing, but on the other hand, the little fish in there will probably hit anything. So kids might get a kick out of it. For swimming, you'll need to pick your spots to get in because the shoreline is shallow and mucky in some spots. On the other hand, motorized craft is banned, so if you can haul a canoe, kayak, inner tube, or some other such thing up there, you can get out on the lake and cruise around.

But back to the wilderness areas. You should certainly stop at the big ranger station in McKenzie Bridge to get maps on the way up, but, without moving your car, you can start at Scott Lake and go 1.5 flat miles to Hand Lake or take the other, slightly tougher trail to Benson Lake (1.5 miles), the Tenas Lakes (3 miles), or 6,116-foot Scott Mountain (4 miles) for some serious views. Just across OR 242, and down 0.5 mile or so, you'll find the Scott Trailhead and the Obsidian Trailhead; both of these trails lead about 5 miles up to the Pacific Crest Trail in a world of unmatched meadows, creeks, and mountain scenery. Much of it lies within the Obsidian Special Permit Area, which requires a permit to spend the night. It's free, but you'll need to get one in advance from the McKenzie River Ranger District.

Even without all that, it's hard to imagine a nicer day in Oregon than hiking around in one of these mountainous wilderness areas, then coming back to Scott Lake and your quiet, peaceful, view-packed campsite. Just don't go in July!

Scott Lake Campground

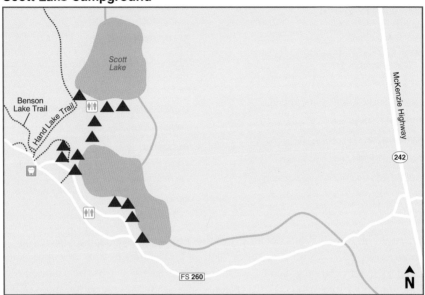

GETTING THERE

From the intersection of US 20 and US 97 in Bend, head west on US 20 for 18.9 miles. In Sisters turn left onto South Pine Street. Immediately turn right onto West Hood Avenue, and go 0.3 mile. Turn left onto OR 242. Drive 20.4 miles and turn left onto Forest Service Road 260. Drive 0.6 mile to the campground.

From I-5 take Exit 194A in Eugene and head east on OR 126. In 48.4 miles turn right onto OR 242 (the turn is about 4.6 miles past McKenzie Bridge). Drive 16 miles and turn left onto FS 260. Drive 0.6 mile to the campground.

GPS COORDINATES: N44° 12.675'   W121° 53.300'

26

Three Creek Lake and Driftwood Campgrounds

Beauty ★★★★★ Privacy ★★★ *(Three Creek Lake)* ★★★★ *(Driftwood)* Spaciousness ★★★★ Quiet ★★★★★
Security ★★★★ Cleanliness ★★★★★

You'll be ensconced in what feels like your own private reserve, with lots of vegetation and tree cover all around.

If you could choose a campsite via aerial surveillance and parachute in for a week, Three Creek Lake and Driftwood would probably top the list. Specifically, we're thinking site 17 at Driftwood, but just about anywhere around Three Creek Lake would suit us fine.

Three Creek Lake is a spectacularly beautiful, high-altitude gem that offers a quality tent-camping experience. It's so great, in fact, that we couldn't quite choose between these two campgrounds, so we're listing both. Driftwood is the nearer to Three Sisters by about a mile (making it a winner in my mind), and Three Creek Lake is at the road's end. Driftwood sprawls around the north shore of Three Creek Lake with 18 sites (12 for tents only). Three Creek Lake is tucked in on the south side with 11 cozy sites. Both campgrounds charge the same fee, both are at the same elevation (6,600'), and both are quite rustic (without piped water but with garbage service).

Three Creek Lake and Tam McArthur Rim

KEY INFORMATION

CONTACT: Hoodoo Recreation Service for Deschutes National Forest, Sisters Ranger District: 541-338-7869, hoodoorecreation .com, www.fs.usda.gov/recarea/deschutes /recreation/camping-cabins/recarea /?recid=38666, www.fs.usda.gov /recarea/deschutes/recreation/camping -cabins/recarea/?recid=38606

OPEN: July–mid-September, depending on snow levels

SITES: Driftwood: 18; Three Creek Lake: 11

WHEELCHAIR ACCESS: Not designated

EACH SITE HAS: Picnic table, fire ring with grill

ASSIGNMENT: First come, first served

REGISTRATION: Self-registration on-site

AMENITIES: Vault toilets, garbage service, no piped water

PARKING: At campsites; $8/additional vehicle

FEE: $16

ELEVATION: 6,600'

RESTRICTIONS:

PETS: On leash only

QUIET HOURS: None specified

FIRES: In fire rings only

ALCOHOL: Permitted

OTHER: RVs up to 20'; no hookups; 14-day stay limit; nonmotorized boats only

Driftwood is accessed off the main road, FS 16, by a short spur to the right. Go for one of the campsites around the farthest perimeter of the lake and you will be ensconced in what feels like your own private reserve, with lots of vegetation and tree cover all around. The drill for these sites is to park your car up above and pack your gear down to the tent site, situated well away from the lake's edge. In fact, most of the sites have their parking space well away from the actual tent-pitching and campfire area. Though you might lose a smidge of convenience, this design is nice because it leaves the immediate surroundings outside your tent in a very natural state.

Sites along the spur road closer to the main road are more open, trading heavy vegetation for more of a beachy feel. It's not unheard of to see anglers on the shore in front of their campsites, relaxing in camp chairs with fishing lines extended out into the lake. Maybe not the most die-hard anglers, but they get their money's worth out of the campsite!

At Three Creek Lake Campground, the sites are arranged on either side of the small loop road. Privacy is not as characteristic here, although all sites share a general feeling of being off the beaten path (well off the path, as a matter of fact). A few sites closer to the lake have the appearance of constant RV wear and tear. Avoid these and choose one of the sites perched on the hillside overlooking the lake. Most people come to Three Creek Lake for the fishing. But with the massive presence of Tam McArthur Rim, which blocks the view of the craggy peaks in the Three Sisters Wilderness just beyond, you know you could be on the brink of a classic alpine adventure. Three Sisters Wilderness is one of the most heavily traveled areas of Central Oregon. It's also one of the larger tracts at 285,202 acres, and because access points from the north tend to be limited to a few spur roads off FS 16, this section of Three Sisters can be surprisingly lonely.

The trailhead for Tam McArthur leaves from Three Creek Lake adjacent to Driftwood Campground, and because you can see where you're headed, the only way out is up. Once you've reached the top of the rim, however, the trail flattens out. The best views of the Three Sisters cluster (North, Middle, and South Sister, as well as Broken Top Mountains) are a little farther along the trail. Numerous link trails will take you to an assortment of alpine lakes and more views of the heart of the Cascades.

Except for the last couple miles of FS 16, the drive up to Driftwood and Three Creek Lake is not particularly eventful or memorable. The valley floor falls away quickly, but what views can be had are mostly in the rearview mirror or filtered through the lodgepole and ponderosa pines that line this highway. Sit back, enjoy the open road in front of you, and hold onto your teeth for the last couple of miles (which can get bumpy in late summer). Then, once you've arrived, have your fill of lake fishing, mountainous hiking, and breathtaking vistas.

Three Creek Lake and Driftwood Campgrounds

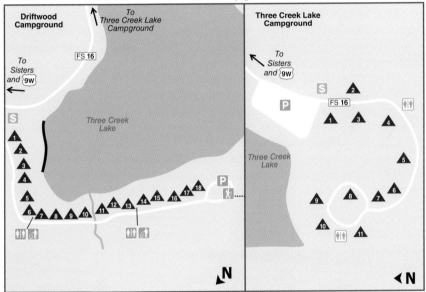

GETTING THERE

From the intersection of US 20 and US 97 in Bend, head west on US 20 for 18.7 miles. In Sisters turn left onto South Elm Street/Three Creek Road/Forest Service Road 16. Drive 16.2 miles up, up, up to the campgrounds. At the fork just before Three Creek Lake, take a right to reach Driftwood Campground.

From I-5 take Exit 233 in Albany and head east on US 20. In 99 miles turn right onto South Elm Street/Three Creek Road/FS 16, and follow the directions above.

GPS COORDINATES:
    THREE CREEK LAKE: N44° 05.729'   W121° 37.351'
    DRIFTWOOD: N44° 06.183'   W121° 37.751'

27

Tumalo State Park Campground

Beauty ★★★ Privacy ★★ Spaciousness ★★★ Quiet ★★ Security ★★★★★ Cleanliness ★★★★

Tumalo makes an ideal base camp for river adventures as well as other expeditions in all directions.

If you're looking for a good base to plant yourself for several days while you explore some of Oregon's best country for outdoor activities, you could do worse than Tumalo State Park. The well-managed compound has excellent facilities, peace of mind when day-tripping, and location, location, location. It's nestled right along the float-friendly Deschutes River and within minutes of the famous Phil's Trail mountain bike network, not to mention all the fine food, beer, and fun to be had in the outdoorsy city of Bend. There's also fishing, backcountry skiing, endless hiking trails, and just hanging out at camp.

For certain, there will be RVs here, but Tumalo does offer a separate tent-camping area (although it could use improvement, if that's the right word). The tent camping loop is to the left of the ranger office as you enter the campground driveway. It's a rather small area, but these sites are closest to the Deschutes River, which makes the environment seem more natural. However, the sites themselves are basic and fairly tight together. As result of their adjacency, they don't offer a lot of privacy, and they have awkwardly situated tent pads in many cases.

Up above in the main camp complex, there are two loops, and, if possible, it's best to grab a spot on the outside loop for more privacy. Don't plan on many spaces being available

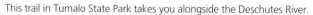

This trail in Tumalo State Park takes you alongside the Deschutes River.

KEY INFORMATION

CONTACT: 541-382-3586, oregonstateparks.org

OPEN: Year-round; hiker/biker and A and C loops closed October–April

SITES: 54 (23 full hookup), 7 yurts, 2 group, 1 hiker/biker camp

WHEELCHAIR ACCESS: Restrooms; sites 11, 19, 20, and 35; yurt 8

EACH SITE HAS: Picnic table, fire ring with grill

ASSIGNMENT: First come, first served, or by reservation (recommended in high season) at 800-452-5687 or reserveamerica.com

REGISTRATION: Self-registration on-site

AMENITIES: Flush toilets, separate solar-powered shower building, playground, amphitheater, firewood, ice

PARKING: At campsites; $7/additional vehicle

FEE: Tent $21, hiker/biker $8, yurt $46; $8 reservation fee

RESTRICTIONS:

PETS: On leash only

QUIET HOURS: 10 p.m.–6 a.m.

FIRES: In fire rings only

ALCOHOL: Permitted at campsites only

OTHER: RVs up to 30'; 14-day stay limit

on short notice on summer weekends. If you know the dates you expect to be in the Bend area, it's best to make a reservation. (Just be sure you're familiar with the very strict cancellation policy in the Oregon campground system when making your reservation.)

Tumalo is also an excellent place to spring for the ultimate luxury in car camping: spending the night in a yurt. Even more than the campsites, though, these tend to book up quickly; you'll want to reserve weeks in advance, if possible.

Whichever option you choose, you're unlikely to find yourself bored around here. Swimming or floating the Deschutes River is something of an Oregon bucket-list item, and given its proximity to the river, Tumalo makes an ideal base camp for river adventures, as well as lots of other expeditions in the area. On a hot day, take the 2-mile trail, which starts at the campground, downriver to discover some excellent opportunities to cool off in the river. Another short trail leads upriver from the recreation area, this one a little rockier but with more shade. And if you're willing to hop in the car for a few minutes, Tumalo acts as a base for any number of longer, more ambitious day hikes; pick up a map at a ranger station before you head out.

Mountain bikers should seek out the trail alongside the Metolius River or the famous Phil's Trail network that laces through the national forest. You're also within easy striking distance of Smith Rock, a necessary stop for any rock climbers in your party and an excellent place from which to admire the evening sunset.

If that's not enough to keep you busy, spend some time in Bend itself. One of Oregon's fastest-growing and most dynamic towns, Bend has a record number of craft breweries per capita in the United States, including some of the state's most iconic beer producers (Deschutes, Boneyard), and its restaurant scene is quickly catching up. The downtown commercial core is compact and easily walkable, inviting exploration; the biggest challenge might be finding a parking spot, as you're unlikely to be the only one here to check out this cool town.

Aside from a surplus of RVs (a plight it shares with just about every developed campground) and an uninspiring tent camping loop, the only notable drawback to Tumalo is the road noise from US 20—part of the price of the convenient-to-everything location. Long-haul trucks ferrying goods east and west across the Cascades travel OR 20 with great regularity—and at all hours of the day and night—and the noise carries over the treetops and above the Deschutes canyon, settling on the campground. On a stiller than still night, the truck sounds are a reminder that Tumalo is not necessarily tent camping at its finest, but maybe at its most convenient. And sometimes that's just what you need.

Tumalo State Park Campground

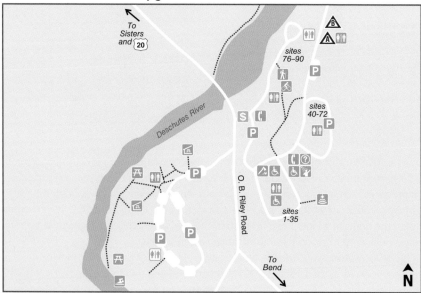

GETTING THERE

From the intersection of US 20 and US 97 in Bend, head west on US 20 for 1.4 miles. Turn left onto Old Bend-Redmond Highway and drive 0.2 mile. Turn right onto O. B. Riley Road (also known as Old McKenzie–Bend Highway), and drive 1.3 miles, including a few sharp corners and sudden drops. (At night, this little stretch of road is surprisingly dark.) The campground entrance is on the right just before crossing the bridge over the Deschutes River.

From I-5 take Exit 233 in Albany and head east on US 20. In 114.4 miles in Bend turn right onto O. B. Riley Road (also known as Old McKenzie–Bend Highway), and drive 1.3 miles, including a few sharp corners and sudden drops. (At night, this little stretch of road is surprisingly dark.) The campground entrance is on the right just after crossing the bridge over the Deschutes River.

GPS COORDINATES: N44° 07.737'   W121° 19.872'

28

⚑ Wildcat Campground

Beauty ★★★ Privacy ★★★★ Spaciousness ★★★★ Quiet ★★★★★ Security ★★★ Cleanliness ★★★

Few other campgrounds afford such close proximity to wilderness or promote such a sense of quietude.

A pleasant drive winds through a scenic little valley dotted with neat ranch houses and summer cabins. A lazy stream wanders along, with lush meadow grasses softening its banks. Cattle graze, birds flit, the road rises gently but steadily around each tree-lined bend, and . . . Whoa, Nellie! What the heck is that?!

The sight of lonely Steins Pillar rising 350 feet above the treetops across the valley is not quite what you'd expect in this otherwise pastoral scene, but there it is. A rather prominent vestige of ancient volcanic activity exposed after millions of years of wear and tear, Steins Pillar seems almost comically out of place. Unlike its counterparts, Twin Pillars and Whistler Peak, it was the unwitting victim of bad location when the 1984 Oregon Wilderness Act formed the Mill Creek Wilderness. All those years standing out there by itself and it turns out to be only 3 miles shy of where they drew the boundary line! It seems a little sad.

You can view Steins Pillar from a wayside pull-over on Mill Creek Road, but there's a fair amount of private land between you and the spire. It takes the right kind of lens to capture the enormity of the pillar on film from this vantage point. If you want to take the detour to view Steins Pillar up close before continuing on up to Wildcat, look for the Steins Pillar sign about a mile past where Mill Creek Road turns to gravel. Turn right, and follow this road sharply up for a little more than 2 miles. The hike in is also about 2 miles and of average difficulty. Bring a water bottle.

Meanwhile, back at the camp . . . Wildcat Campground is another 5 miles up Mill Creek Road and sits at the intersection of Mill Creek proper and its East Fork. The southwest boundary of the Mill Creek Wilderness is veritably at your tent's backflap. There are few other campgrounds in this book that afford such close proximity to wilderness or promote such a sense of quietude. Campsites here are arranged in a loop with a blend of high desert grasses, aspen, and pines against a backdrop of sun-browned canyon slopes. With the East Fork of Mill Creek babbling through, it's quite a pretty yet primitive setting. The locals will tell you this is one of the best places to cool off

Take a detour on the way to Wildcat Campground for an up close view of Steins Pillar. *(courtesy of the U.S. Forest Service–Pacific Northwest Region/public domain)*

KEY INFORMATION

CONTACT: Ochoco National Forest: 541-416-6500, www.fs.usda.gov/recarea/ochoco/recarea/?recid=38776

OPEN: Mid-April–mid-October

SITES: 17

WHEELCHAIR ACCESS: Not designated

EACH SITE HAS: Picnic table, fire ring with grill

ASSIGNMENT: First come, first served

REGISTRATION: Self-registration on-site

AMENITIES: Vault toilets, piped water

PARKING: At some campsites and at access road, 200–400 yards from campground; $7/additional vehicle

FEE: $15

ELEVATION: 3,700'

RESTRICTIONS:

PETS: On leash only

QUIET HOURS: None specified

FIRES: In fire rings only

ALCOHOL: Permitted

OTHER: RVs longer than 20' not recommended; no hookups; 14-day stay limit

from the searing desert heat down below—something you'll be able to vouch for if you've driven in across east Central Oregon's John Day River basin.

The higher you go, the cooler it will get. And the fewer people you'll find. The Mill Creek Wilderness is minuscule by comparison to most of Oregon's other wild lands, but it is the largest of three in the Ochoco Range (Bridge Creek and Black Canyon are the others). Despite this and its modest notoriety for quizzical rock formations, the Mill Creek Wilderness is often overlooked by residents of the Bend/Redmond/Prineville metropolis, who typically migrate west into the Cascades or even farther east into the heart of the Blue Mountains instead. The rock-climbing crowd has turned its fascination northwest to Smith Rock outside Terrebonne, and that reduces the public pressure on Mill Creek's attractions as well.

Given the small stature of the wilderness, its 21 miles of trails can be traversed in no time. On the other hand, once you're here, you might consider taking the opportunity to dawdle since you're not required to canvass the land in record time. You'll get reasonable exercise, though, with three main trails in the system linking to each other in a range of elevations from 3,700 feet (at the campground) to as high as 6,200 feet.

And although it's cooler than the stifling desert, it's still plenty hot and dry, so carry a lot of water.

A word of warning about the East Fork of Mill Creek and its tributaries while on the subject of water: Don't drink from the stream unless you have a water purifier or filtration system. (A good rule no matter where you are, really.) It may look innocent enough—and how easy it would be to scoop up a palmful while you're heading up the trail to Twin Pillars. But keep in mind that free-ranging cattle are allowed inside the boundaries of Mill Creek and they have proven to be a nuisance to the natural environment, including contaminating the water.

Hopefully, you'll see more wildlife than cattle in your rambles through Mill Creek Wilderness. It's likely that you will, as the level of human traffic is not heavy enough to make native creatures unduly wary. You'd probably rather not run into a black bear or mountain lion (although both live here), but you may be lucky enough to glimpse elk, mule deer, and a variety of birds—the pileated woodpecker thrives on fallen old-growth ponderosas here, and wild turkeys roam the lower elevations.

Wildcat Campground

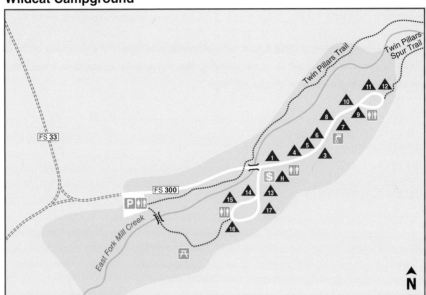

GETTING THERE

From the intersection of US 20 and US 97 in Bend, head north on US 97 for 12.9 miles to Redmond. Turn right onto OR 126 E and drive 17.8 miles to Prineville. Merge onto US 26 E and drive 9.9 miles. Turn left onto Mill Creek Road/Forest Service Road 33. Drive 10.6 miles to the campground.

From I-5 take Exit 233 in Albany and head east on US 20. In 99.7 miles turn left onto OR 126 E, and go 18.8 miles. Turn left onto US 97, and in 0.3 mile turn right to get on OR 126 again. Drive 17.8 miles to Prineville. Merge onto US 26 E and drive 9.9 miles. Turn left onto Mill Creek Road/FS 33. Drive 10.6 miles to the campground.

GPS COORDINATES: N44° 26.399'   W120° 34.803'

29

Yellowbottom Campground

Beauty ★★★★★ Privacy ★★★ Spaciousness ★★★★ Quiet ★★★★ Security ★★ Cleanliness ★★★★★

The Quartzville Corridor is truly a gold mine (literally and figuratively), laden with opportunity whether your visit is an overnight gathering around a campfire, a week lost among old-growth giants, or a lifetime of trips.

If you plan to camp at Yellowbottom and you want to take the scenic route first, come in from the US 22 connector on FS 11. This brings you along the ridge-running, breathtaking Quartzville Back Country Byway, reportedly one of the least-traveled byways in Oregon.

The Quartzville Creek Corridor is impressive due to the fact that a collection of public and private interests work cooperatively to manage this region. What other 50-mile stretch qualifies as dam-controlled, wild and scenic, historic, and recreational under the auspices of five different agencies? This alone is a modern miracle.

Yellowbottom Campground sits nearly equidistant from both ends of the Quartzville Byway and is the only developed campground within the wild and scenic portion of Quartzville Creek, falling under the Bureau of Land Management jurisdiction. Wedged into the right angle formed by Yellowbottom Creek falling from the north and Quartzville Creek running in an east–west parallel with the road, the campground has 22 sites laid out in an

Relax on the shores of Quartzville Creek.
(courtesy of the Bureau of Land Management Oregon and Washington/Flickr/CC BY 2.0 [creativecommons.org/licenses/by/2.0])

KEY INFORMATION

CONTACT: Bureau of Land Management: 503-375-5646, blm.gov/visit /quartzville-back-country-byway

OPEN: Mid-May–early September

SITES: 22

WHEELCHAIR ACCESS: Not designated

EACH SITE HAS: Picnic table, fire ring with grill

ASSIGNMENT: First come, first served

REGISTRATION: Self-registration on-site

AMENITIES: Vault toilets, piped water, garbage service, firewood

PARKING: At sites; 2 vehicles/site; overflow parking available; $7/additional vehicle

FEE: $12

ELEVATION: 1,500'

RESTRICTIONS:

PETS: On leash only

QUIET HOURS: 10 p.m.–7 a.m.

FIRES: In fire rings only

ALCOHOL: Permitted

OTHER: 14-day stay limit; no gathered wood more than 1 inch in diameter; entrance gate locked 10 p.m.–7 a.m.

intelligent use of the natural geography. It is hard to find a site that seems inappropriate or awkwardly placed. The entire compound simultaneously evokes backcountry wilderness and a sense of order that is classic Bureau of Land Management (BLM)—something to do with that "less is more" approach to recreational resources.

Even so, this must be one of the more developed BLM campgrounds in the state. One would have to refer to Yellowbottom as practically upscale in comparison to most of the agency's campgrounds, and this is where the sense of order is evident. There is a woodshed for firewood, a pump house for water, a power building, and even a small cabin from which the camp host (who is usually on-site for the month of August only) distributes literature. Across the Quartzville Road from the overnight camping is the day-use/picnic area, which can be a bit of a hubbub on a sultry summer afternoon. Word has spread of the spectacular swimming hole on the Quartzville here. Bodies sprawl on every available sun-warmed rock surface after a quick plunge in becomes an even quicker scramble out. Quartzville Creek is clear, clear, clear but cold, cold, cold.

Although the campground sports an unusually high level of organization, the basic amenities (two sets of vault toilets) are not exactly situated in the best proximity to most of the campsites (it can be a long walk in the middle of the night, in other words). The same goes for the piped water. While the best sites for privacy are those backed up against the north slope of the campground (4, 5, 6, 8, 9, and 11), they are also the ones where you'll want to consider filling up one container and emptying another (if you get our meaning) before the campfire dies out.

Old-growth fir, western red cedar, and rhododendron are the most noticeable permanent residents around Yellowbottom. The Rhododendron Trail, which loops around the north side of the campground boundary, is evidence of their peaceful coexistence and can be observed up close on a short but robust hike. Longer hikes are not far away in the petite and little-traveled Middle Santiam Wilderness. If you don't make it there on this trip, be sure you put it on your list of things to do sometime next year. The trailhead into the northern sector of the Middle Santiam is accessed off of FS 1142, a right turn not more than 2 miles east of Yellowbottom.

The Quartzville Corridor is truly a gold mine (literally and figuratively), laden with opportunity whether your visit is an afternoon drive, a day picking huckleberries, an overnight gathering around a campfire, a week lost among old-growth giants, or a lifetime of trips, each with something different to offer. Gold mining put this area on the map once and still lures today's amateur fortune hunters. Primarily, however, it has become the domain of anglers, boaters, hikers, and berry pickers. For the future, let's hope the legacies we have kept alive and the ones we have created inspire those who follow us.

Yellowbottom Campground

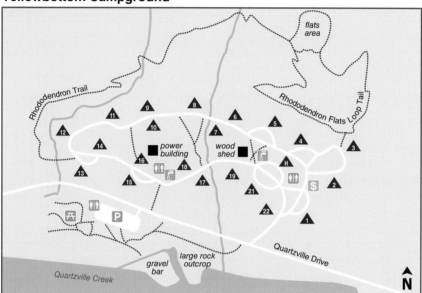

GETTING THERE

From the intersection of US 20 and US 97 in Bend, head west on US 20 for 44.4 miles. Head right on OR 22 W, and go 12.5 miles. Turn left onto Straight Creek Road/Forest Service Road 11, and go 24.3 miles. Continue straight onto Quartzille Drive, and go another 1.5 miles to the campground, which will be on your right. A day-use area and Quartzville Creek are on your left.

From I-5 take Exit 233 in Albany and head east on US 20. Go 31.8 miles, and turn left onto Quartzville Drive. In 23.6 miles the campground will be on your left. A day-use area and Quartzville Creek are on your right.

GPS COORDINATES: N44° 35.385'   W122° 22.368'

SOUTHERN CASCADES

Toketee Falls near Susan Creek Campground (see page 122)

30

Crater Lake National Park: Lost Creek Campground

Beauty ★★★★ Privacy ★★★★★ Spaciousness ★★★★★ Quiet ★★★★★ Security ★★★ Cleanliness ★★★★

Oregon's only national park, now nearly 120 years old, retains the stupendous natural wonders that garnered its protection in 1902.

There's one thing to know about Lost Creek Campground: get there as early as possible and stake your claim. Bribe someone if you have to.

Here's the deal: Lost Creek is one of only two campgrounds inside the boundary of Crater Lake National Park. And with 16 tent-only sites—compared to Mazama's 214 multipurpose sites—the odds are not in a latecomer's favor. Even though Lost Creek is a bit off the beaten path, the area is swarming with people looking for overnight accommodations—roughly half a million visitors per year at last count. Many of them come from around the world, and it's easy to see why: Crater Lake is an unparalleled sight, impossible to overhype. One glimpse and you'll catch your breath; gaze around a little longer and it just gets better.

Oregon's only national park, now nearly 120 years old, retains the stupendous natural wonders that garnered its protection in 1902. Park staff have said that William Steel, the singular driving force behind the park's creation, would be impressed with how little Crater Lake has changed in the course of a century. Other than the paving of formerly dirt roads, the only evident change is at Crater Lake Lodge, which underwent a multimillion-dollar remodeling in the early 1990s.

If this is your first trip to Crater Lake National Park, be prepared. Your jaw will drop when you take your first peek over the rim of this massive caldera. Everyone has an opinion on the best spot for your first good gawk, but frankly, that's just splitting hairs. The deepest lake in the United States, the second deepest in North America, and one of the 10 deepest in the world, Crater Lake is the result of the cataclysmic eruption of Mount Mazama some 7,700 years ago. It once was a stratovolcano similar to Mount Hood and Mount Shasta and stood roughly a

Crater Lake emerges from its shroud of mist with a view of Wizard Island.

KEY INFORMATION

CONTACT: 541-594-3000, nps.gov/crla /planyourvisit/lost_creek.htm

OPEN: July–mid-October, depending on snow levels

SITES: 16

WHEELCHAIR ACCESS: Fully accessible campground

EACH SITE HAS: Picnic table, fire ring with grill, bear-proof food lockers

ASSIGNMENT: First come, first served

REGISTRATION: Self-registration on-site

AMENITIES: Flush toilets, no piped water

PARKING: At campsites

FEE: $10

ELEVATION: 6,000'

RESTRICTIONS:

PETS: On leash and with permit only

QUIET HOURS: None specified

FIRES: In fire rings only

ALCOHOL: Permitted at campsites only

OTHER: Motorbikes allowed; no accommodations for RVs

mile higher than the current lake level before it collapsed. Pick up brochures about Crater Lake, Mount Mazama, and the park at one of the two visitor centers before you tour the area. This is the kind of place where a little knowledge can make the trip more pleasurable.

Rim Drive circumnavigates the perimeter of the 6-mile-wide lake for a total distance of 33.4 miles. There are numerous viewpoints along the way where you'll want to stop and take photos, but give yourself roughly 2 hours to drive around the loop. In the winter, Rim Drive is open only between park headquarters and Rim Village, accessed by way of OR 62 from either the west or the south. In all seasons, Rim Drive is open to bicycles, but there is no shoulder—so be careful!

Recreational activities in the 183,277 acres of Crater Lake National Park border on exhaustive, but the wanderer in you may want to simply observe on foot the diverse plant and animal life native to this part of Oregon. There are more than 140 miles of hiking trails (including a section of the Pacific Crest Trail), and with so many of the park's visitors limiting their activity to areas closest to the crater's rim and park services, it is relatively easy to find solitude on a trail. Some trails reach elevations close to 9,000 feet and can take their toll on unconditioned legs and the unacclimatized cardiovascular system. Remember to carry water and take frequent rest stops to adjust to the altitude—and the incredibly fresh air.

For the geologist in you, there are destinations such as The Pinnacles (farther down the road from Lost Creek Camp) and similarly weird formations on the Godfrey Glen Trail. The Pumice Desert is on the north side of the park, and Wizard Island, the small, symmetrical volcanic cone protruding from the lake, is accessible by boat from Cleetwood Cove. It's a steep, 720-foot drop on a trail just over a mile long to hike to the cove. The way down may seem manageable enough, but after several hours of hiking on Wizard Island, that last mile back up may be a bit challenging. Leave enough time to make the ascent in daylight.

Though access is more limited, winter at Crater Lake is the dominant season, starting as early as October and lasting well into what is early summer in most places. Annual snowfall averages around 500 inches, which means endless winter-recreation opportunities, if you're prepared. The park offers marked (but not groomed) cross-country skiing trails and snowmobile options. Most services in the park close in winter, but the café and gift shop at Rim Village stay open daily. Check the park's website for the most current conditions when considering a winter escape.

Crater Lake National Park: Lost Creek Campground

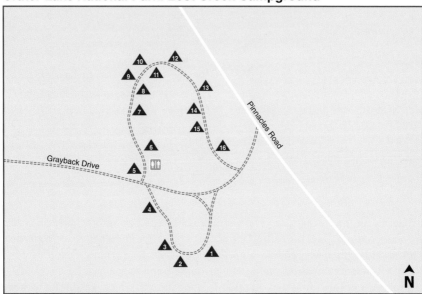

GETTING THERE

From I-5 take Exit 30 in Medford (OR 62 E/OR 238 W/North Medford). Head east on OR 62 (from northbound, a right turn; from southbound, a left turn). Drive 54.5 miles, then turn right to stay on OR 62 E. Drive 15.8 miles, then turn left onto Munson Valley Road/Volcanic Legacy Scenic Byway (the Annie Spring Entrance to Crater Lake National Park). Drive 3.9 miles, then turn right onto Rim Drive/Volcanic Legacy Scenic Byway and drive 8.2 miles. Turn right onto Pinnacles Road (if you're still on East Rim Drive and you see the Phantom Ship Overlook on your left, you've gone just a bit too far). Drive 3.1 miles to the intersection with Grayback Drive. Lost Creek Campground is adjacent to tiny Lost Creek on the right.

GPS COORDINATES: N42° 52.793'   W122° 02.316'

31

Fourmile Lake Campground

Beauty ★★★★ Privacy ★★★ Spaciousness ★★★★★ Quiet ★★★★ Security ★★★★ Cleanliness ★★★★★

If you're campground shopping in the southern Oregon Cascades, it's hard to beat these fabulous views, lakefront sites, and wilderness trails.

Get ready for views of a 9,500-foot snowcapped peak, spacious lakefront tent sites wonderfully free of annoying mosquitoes (well, for most of the year), a wilderness boundary practically at the backflap of your tent, trailheads to some of the wildest high-elevation territory in Oregon, a vast national wildlife refuge less than 20 miles away, regular security patrols, and the services of civilization within an hour's drive. It's hard to beat this glowing set of credentials, which is all part of the package when you stay at Fourmile Lake Campground in Fremont-Winema National Forest.

Although Fourmile's campsites are sizable enough to accommodate RVs, the general sense of the place is one of solitude and serenity. This is due, in part, to the proximity of Sky Lakes Wilderness, the boundary of which is outlined by nearly three-fourths of the lake's shoreline.

Creating this squiggly crook in the wilderness's otherwise linear demarcation, Fourmile Lake is not within the protected boundaries, and motorized boat travel (with enforced speed limits) is acceptable. Any form of mechanized transportation within the wilderness territory is, however, strictly prohibited.

As always when hiking into wilderness backcountry, it is a good idea to carry a compass and a detailed USGS topographic map of the area. U.S. Forest Service maps are generally reliable but are often not updated frequently enough to reflect the most recent additions or

Mount McLoughlin looms large behind Fourmile Lake Campground.

KEY INFORMATION

CONTACT: Fremont-Winema National Forest, Klamath Ranger District: 541-885-3400, www.fs.usda.gov/recarea/fremont-winema/recarea/?recid=59727

OPEN: Late June–mid-October, weather permitting

SITES: 29

WHEELCHAIR ACCESS: Toilets, 2 sites, picnic area, boat ramp

EACH SITE HAS: Picnic table, fire ring with grill

ASSIGNMENT: First come, first served

REGISTRATION: Self-registration on-site

AMENITIES: Vault toilets, central hand pumps for water, boat launch

PARKING: At campsites; $6/additional vehicle

FEE: $15

ELEVATION: 5,750'

RESTRICTIONS:

PETS: On leash only

QUIET HOURS: 10 p.m.–6 a.m.

FIRES: In fire rings only

ALCOHOL: Permitted

OTHER: No vehicles allowed in wilderness area; 14-day stay limit

changes in their vast network of roads. Try to get the most current information from a U.S. Forest Service representative. They're very friendly and helpful in Klamath Falls.

Hiking is required to get the most out of this area, so carefully consider your options in either Sky Lakes Wilderness or Mountain Lakes Wilderness. Trails into Sky Lakes begin very near the campground. The one to the northwest passes diminutive Squaw Lake (where views of Mount McLoughlin will make you stop and gawk) and soon thereafter connects with the Pacific Crest Trail (PCT) about 2 miles from the campground. From there, you could hike south on the PCT to its junction with the Mount McLoughlin Trail (a difficult but nontechnical climb). The summit is about 3 miles from this point. The trip from campground to peak would make for a rather rigorous 14-mile, round-trip day hike. The alternative is to hike the Mount McLoughlin Trail from its trailhead on FS 3650. An elevation gain of 4,000 feet doesn't make the trip any easier, but it is shorter (10 miles round-trip). Be sure to read the brochure that is provided at the trailhead. It covers some necessary precautions that can make the difference between delight and disaster on this fourth-highest Oregon Cascade volcano.

To experience the true essence of Sky Lakes Wilderness, I recommend driving to the Cold Springs trailhead on FS 3651. Saunter into the heart of this magnificent area with Imagination Peak as your inspiration. Beginning at an altitude of 5,800 feet, the trail climbs gently up and down without general elevation gain or loss.

In about 6 miles, you'll come to Heavenly Twin Lakes and the turnaround point if you're just out for the day. This is a good spot to see osprey that travel from nesting areas up to 8 miles away to fish in the hundreds of lakes scattered in this alpine basin. The trail wanders north past more peaks and lakes until it catches up with the PCT as it works its way toward Crater Lake National Park.

Southeast of Fourmile Lake is Mountain Lakes Wilderness, one of the oldest designated wilderness areas in Oregon and, for that matter, the entire country. The U.S. Forest Service included it in its primitive areas designations back in the 1930s, and it was incorporated under the 1964 Wilderness Act. Lesser known than the more popular destinations to the north but quite accessible from a trailhead at Sunset Campground, it may be the ticket for those seeking more solitary environs.

A challenging side trip—if you have the four-wheel rig to make it—is up Pelican Butte (also accessed from FS 3651). The U.S. Forest Service once manned a lookout station here, but the road is not maintained for normal-clearance vehicles. Currently, Pelican Butte is officially designated as an 11,000-acre roadless area, but a wilderness status is pending. No word on when this may be approved, but there is no doubt it would be a good thing for nature lovers.

Of course, hiking is not the only way to see this spectacular region. Rent a canoe down on Pelican Bay and follow Upper Klamath Canoe Trail through 6 miles of lake and marshland. An array of wildlife and waterfowl inhabits the 15,000 acres that comprise the Klamath National Wildlife Refuge.

Fourmile Lake Campground

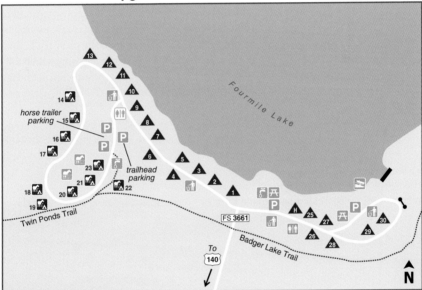

GETTING THERE

From I-5 take Exit 30 in Medford (OR 62 E/OR 238 W/North Medford). Head east on OR 62 (from northbound, a right turn; from southbound, a left turn). Drive 5.6 miles, and turn right onto OR 140/Lake of the Woods Highway. In 32.4 miles turn left onto Forest Service Road 3650, and go 2.6 miles. Turn left onto Fourmile Lake Road/FS 3661. The campground will be on your right in 2.7 miles.

From the intersection of US 97 and OR 140 in Klamath Falls, take OR 140 W and drive 33 miles. Turn right onto Fourmile Lake Road/FS 3661 and drive 5.6 miles to the campground, on your right.

GPS COORDINATES: N42° 27.274'   W122° 14.841'

32

Head of the River Campground

Beauty ★★★★ Privacy ★★ Spaciousness ★★★★ Quiet ★★★★ Security ★ Cleanliness ★★★

Here's a great little out-of-the-way place where you'll run into more wildlife than people.

You know those campgrounds the locals are afraid to tell anyone about, in case the whole world finds out they exist? Head of the River Campground is (was? sorry) one of those places. Sure, it shows up on official U.S. Forest Service lists—but this is about as out-of-the-way as a campground can possibly be. You'd be unlikely to venture out here if someone hadn't recommended it at some point. On the other hand, it's really only about 50 miles from Crater Lake, not a bad drive if you're in the area already (and, needless to say, a gorgeous one). And it's about 100 miles from Ashland, 150 from Eugene, and 65 from Klamath Falls, just to add a little perspective. It's not so far after all, especially once you know what awaits you there.

The main lure for campers at this tableland of ponderosa pine, lodgepole pine, and other conifers is the excellent trout fishing in the Williamson River, plus a crazy contingent of U.S. Forest Service roads wandering in and around the numerous buttes and flats. The U.S. Forest Service would like to encourage more recreational use of these roads, which are primarily used by loggers, but it doesn't really have the resources to promote it as such. Which means intrepid campers who venture beyond the more populated recreation areas may be pleasantly surprised.

This region is relatively dry year-round, and the only substantial precipitation comes in the form of snow at higher elevations. However, enough groundwater seeps to the surface

Lily pads and grasses feed the various inhabitants of Klamath Marsh National Wildlife Refuge.
(courtesy of the U.S. Forest Service–Pacific Northwest Region/public domain)

KEY INFORMATION

CONTACT: Fremont-Winema National Forest, Klamath Ranger District: 541-783-4001, www.fs.usda.gov/recarea /fremont-winema/recarea/?recid=59721

OPEN: Year-round (not maintained mid-October–mid-May)

SITES: 5

WHEELCHAIR ACCESS: Vault toilet, 1 site

EACH SITE HAS: Picnic table

ASSIGNMENT: First come, first served

REGISTRATION: None

AMENITIES: Vault toilet, firewood, no potable water

PARKING: At campsites

FEE: None

ELEVATION: 4,200'

RESTRICTIONS:

PETS: On leash only

QUIET HOURS: None specified

FIRES: In fire rings only

ALCOHOL: Permitted

OTHER: RVs up to 30'

from natural springs (this is precisely the case with the headwaters of the Williamson) that wildflowers, such as fireweed, foxglove, lupine, and dandelion, define the banks of tiny, short-lived creeks every spring.

You'll most likely encounter more wildlife than fellow campers out here. More than 230 species of birds and 80 varieties of mammals inhabit the region. In the summer months, watch out for rattlesnakes and bring your mosquito repellent. Carry your own drinking water to Head of the River or be prepared to treat what you take from the river.

Rather than backtracking along the route you take to reach this pristine spot, consider a loop trip by continuing north on Williamson River Road, which runs into Silver Lake Road just above the expansive Klamath Marsh. You can get a close-up view of Klamath National Wildlife Refuge because Silver Lake Road cuts a diagonal across the refuge's midsection to a juncture with US 97. The 40,000-acre refuge was established in 1958 as a protected sanctuary for migratory birds, and today the Oregon Department of Fish and Wildlife runs the refuge in consultation with the Klamath tribes that gave it its name. It's a remarkable area to drive through—we say this a lot, but you'll want to bring a camera. (Of course, it should go without saying that you'll also need a map and a full tank of gas before setting out, and you should top up at every opportunity, just to be safe. This could easily be one of the least-traveled byways you'll find in this book, or in the state.) Klamath Marsh has a lot to offer, including fishing, hunting, canoeing, and kayaking—your best bet is probably to stop off at the wildlife refuge's headquarters first (21401 Silver Lake Road), for the latest conditions, recommendations, and tips on what to look for and where. Call the center at 541-783-3380 to make sure staff will be available, as hours are varied and limited. Fishing and bird-watching are the biggest draws here—bird species to look for include sandhill cranes and several types of nesting ducks. It's a stunning, wide-open area to drive through, regardless of the season.

All in all, this is a remote place that begs to be appreciated simply for . . . well, its simplicity. The campground is as primitive as they come, with only a handful of sites, no piped water, and no fee. For more specifics on things to do while in the area, check either with the Chiloquin or Klamath Ranger District.

Head of the River Campground

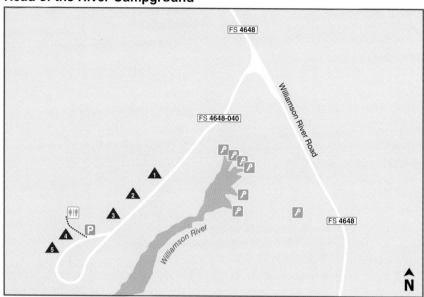

GETTING THERE

From the intersection of US 97 and OR 140 in Klamath Falls, head north on US 97. Drive 29.3 miles, and take Exit 247 (Chiloquin/Crater Lake). Turn right onto OR 422 E and drive 1.4 miles. Turn left onto North First Avenue, which quickly becomes Sprague River Road/ County Road 858, and drive 5.3 miles. Turn left onto Williamson River Road and drive 7.5 miles. Turn left to remain on Williamson, and go another 5.3 miles. Turn left again to stay on Williamson, and go 11.5 miles. Turn left onto Forest Service Road 4648 and follow signs from here; drive 0.5 mile to the campground on the left.

GPS COORDINATES: N42° 43.946'   W121° 25.107'

33

Natural Bridge Campground

Beauty ★★★★★ Privacy ★★★★★ Spaciousness ★★★ Quiet ★★★★ Security ★★★★ Cleanliness ★★★★★

The Upper Rogue River area offers its own style of spectacular scenery and wilderness treasures.

Often overlooked by travelers scurrying between the heavily promoted majesty of Crater Lake and the famed lower Wild and Scenic Rogue River, the Upper Rogue River area offers its own style of spectacular scenery and wilderness treasures that should satisfy the desires of most outdoor adventurers.

If you're set on experiencing the beauty of the Rogue by boat, however, you'll be disappointed to discover that this section of the river is off limits to kayaks and canoes. Head on down to Grants Pass or the town of Rogue River, and they'll take care of you there.

Here, in Upper Rogue territory, the river plummets out of its source in Crater Lake National Park at a rate of as much as 48 feet per mile. Take a look down from precipitous heights along OR 62 north of Natural Bridge Campground for perhaps the clearest indication of why this portion of the river is not runnable. The flash of silver far below is the Rogue hurling itself seaward through the deep, narrow fissure known as the Rogue River Gorge.

Natural Bridge Campground is so named for the unique geological feature adjacent to it. In this location, the Upper Rogue disappears from sight and runs through an underground

Campgrounds along the Upper Rogue River offer lush scenery and easy access to some of the river's unique formations.

KEY INFORMATION

CONTACT: Rogue River National Forest, High Cascades Ranger District: 541-560-3400, www.fs.usda.gov/recarea/rogue-siskiyou/recarea/?recid=69828

OPEN: Late May–early November, depending on snow levels

SITES: 17

WHEELCHAIR ACCESS: Not designated

EACH SITE HAS: Picnic table, fire ring with grill

ASSIGNMENT: First come, first served

REGISTRATION: None

AMENITIES: Vault toilets, no piped water

PARKING: At campsites; $5/additional vehicle

FEE: $10

ELEVATION: 2,900'

RESTRICTIONS:

PETS: On leash only

QUIET HOURS: 10 p.m.–6 a.m.

FIRES: In fire rings only

ALCOHOL: Permitted

OTHER: RVs up to 22'

channel for 200 feet. The campground sits virtually atop the channel, with water flowing beneath it. A 2-mile interpretive loop trail explains the phenomenon.

Natural Bridge is one of several campgrounds in the vicinity located on the banks of the Rogue or on small creeks that feed it. Given its proximity to Crater Lake, this area can be quite busy in the summertime, but the larger, more developed campsites tend to fill up first. The lack of piped water or hookups at Natural Bridge discourages those who are not prepared for primitive conditions. The surrounding Rogue River National Forest is characterized by dense forests of Douglas fir and sugar pine, which soften the contours of the high plateau upon which they grow. More than 450 miles of trail within the national forest lead to remote high-country lakes, ridgetop vistas, and the secluded Rogue–Umpqua Divide Wilderness. Some of the routes connect with trails into the adjoining Umpqua National Forest.

Numerous day hikes and extended backpacking trips reveal not only the natural splendor of this undisturbed country but also the diverse wildlife and plant species that thrive in the moderate climate. The most famous inhabitant of Upper Rogue country is the northern spotted owl, which shares this lush expanse with an astonishing assortment of nocturnal creatures.

Except at the highest altitudes, which receive sizable measures of snow in the winter and stay cool year-round, the area enjoys warm and dry summers, with most of the 20–40 inches of annual precipitation occurring between October and May.

This rugged land is full of thick vegetation. Getting lost is easy. Make sure you have a good topographic or U.S. Forest Service map with you when you head out for lonely and distant spots. Booklets of maps and trail guides are available at the Rogue River National Forest headquarters in Medford or at the district office in Prospect.

If you are looking for an ambitious overland trek, take the Upper Rogue River Trail, which follows the river along its banks for 48 miles until it intersects with the Pacific Crest Trail in Crater Lake National Park. Starting in Prospect, the Upper Rogue Trail does not seem to attract as much print attention as its lower counterpart, known officially as the Rogue River National Recreation Trail. There's very little mention of the upper trail in regional guidebooks, so check in at the ranger station in Prospect, which is the best source for all outdoor recreation options in the area.

You can explore the trail in sections. (Who has time for a 48-mile, all-in-one trip anyway?) If you do have the time (and two cars or some kind of shuttle option), tackle the entire stretch and make daily destinations of the campgrounds sprinkled along the way, Natural Bridge included. This would be a fine way to spend a week getting intimately acquainted with the best of Upper Rogue country. Other options include shorter trails within a couple miles of the campground: The Natural Bridge Interpretive Trail (0.3 mile) along the river often showcases beaver ponds. The Rogue Gorge Interpretive Trail (0.5 mile) also includes fascinating pothole formations in the rock, caused by the continuous spinning of small rocks in the water. And the Union Creek Trail (4.4 miles) follows the creek through a flower-filled old-growth Douglas fir forest to Union Falls.

Natural Bridge Campground

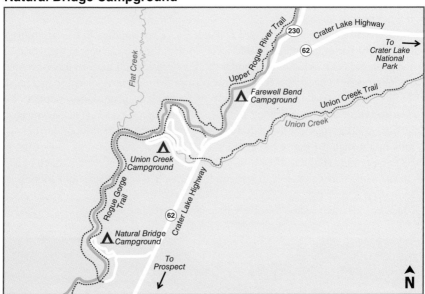

GETTING THERE

From I-5 take Exit 30 in Medford (OR 62 E/OR 238 W/North Medford). Head east on OR 62 (from northbound, a right turn; from southbound, a left turn). Drive 52.1 miles, then turn left onto Forest Service Road 300. Drive 0.4 mile to the campground.

GPS COORDINATES: N42° 53.551'   W122° 27.770'

34

Sacandaga Campground

Beauty ★★★★★ Privacy ★★★★ Spaciousness ★★★★★ Quiet ★★★★★ Security ★★★★ Cleanliness ★★★★★

Waldo Lake, Diamond Peak, and the Willamette River are all within easy reach of Sacandaga.

The area surrounding Oakridge and Westfir is a forest playground for the outdoors-oriented masses of the Eugene-Springfield area. It is also becoming quite well known (thanks in part to effective self-promotion) as a mountain-biking destination in the world beyond Oregon, but don't expect a hip, lively scene—it's still a quaint little town in the middle of nowhere. The number of churches outweighs the tavern listings on the visitor's map, if that tells you anything.

Oakridge is also a jumping-off point to High Cascades wonders in the southern Willamette National Forest, including Waldo Lake—one of the purest lakes in the world—and majestic Diamond Peak. Sacandaga Campground is close enough to town for conveniences but far enough away to be serene. It's safely away from the sometimes-rowdy campers along nearby Hills Creek Reservoir and is definitely less overrun than supremely popular Waldo Lake, yet it's within day-tour driving distance of the High Cascades. At Sacandaga, the Middle Fork Willamette cuts through a narrow canyon that is seemingly far below but still emits up through the dense forest of Douglas fir, cedar, and hemlock one of the most pleasant campground sounds—the soothing constancy of a rushing river. A steep trail leads down to the river; walk cautiously in wet conditions, as it is easy to lose your footing.

At 180 feet long, the Office Bridge in Westfir is the longest covered bridge in Oregon.
(courtesy of the U.S. Forest Service–Pacific Northwest Region/public domain)

KEY INFORMATION

CONTACT: Willamette National Forest, Middle Fork Ranger District: 541-782-2283, www.fs.usda.gov/recarea/willamette /recarea/?recid=4510

OPEN: Mid-June–October

SITES: 16

WHEELCHAIR ACCESS:
Not designated

EACH SITE HAS: Picnic table, fire ring

ASSIGNMENT: First come, first served

REGISTRATION: Self-registration on-site

AMENITIES: Vault toilets, hand-pumped water, garbage service

PARKING: At campsites; $4/additional vehicle

FEE: $8

ELEVATION: 2,400'

RESTRICTIONS:

PETS: On leash only

QUIET HOURS: 10 p.m.–6 a.m.

FIRES: In fire rings only

ALCOHOL: Permitted

OTHER: Trailers up to 24'; 14-day stay limit; no chain saws

At the campground, you'll find beautifully spacious campsites beneath a deep-forest canopy interspersed with dogwood trees. In our estimation, campsites 4, 6, and 8 are the best. Each sits on the edge of the bluff high above the river, the best vantage point for views and the sounds of the river right outside your tent door. Back in to your campsite, unload in relative privacy, and, except for the occasional trip to the water faucet or the vault toilet, you can choose to have very little contact with other campers. Chances are good that these sites will be available, as the U.S. Forest Service rates this campground as seeing "low" usage, but you really can't go wrong anywhere within the camp if you don't get one of the prime spots.

Great driving tours are within easy reach of Sacandaga Campground, but one of the best tours can be enjoyed via foot, pedal, or hoof power right from the campground. The 27-mile-long Middle Fork Trail meanders through old-growth stands and meadows up and around the river, ending at the headwaters of its eponymous creek at Timpanogas Lake. The trail is open to hikers, horses, and mountain bikers; the lower part of the trail is considered a good introduction to serious mountain biking, with enough roots, rocks, and short climbs to challenge (but not discourage) a beginner. It also makes a great hike that even the youngest member of your party can enjoy. Sacandaga sits a little less than halfway along the trail, so you can choose routes in either direction.

Sections of the Middle Fork Trail follow the old Oregon Central Military Wagon Road, originally built in 1864 to bring cattle from the Willamette Valley over Emigrant Pass to the southern and eastern portions of the state. (It was eventually replaced by what is now OR 58 over Willamette Pass). The campground lies along the Diamond Drive Tour, which also follows part of the Military Wagon Road. The route stretches south from Oakridge to OR 138 along the Rogue-Umpqua Scenic Byway, and provides excellent views of Diamond Peak, Mount Thielsen, and Sawtooth Mountain. Diamond Drive also connects on its north end to FS 19, also known as Aufderheide Memorial Drive. (The Aufderheide is also part of the southern leg of the West Cascade Scenic Byway.) The Aufderheide tour starts near the longest covered bridge in Oregon, located in Westfir, and climbs along the rugged North Fork of the Middle Fork of the Willamette River, to the McKenzie River and OR 126 (see Frissell Crossing, page 70, for more information on the Aufderheide).

Closer to the Oakridge end of FS 21, an alternative camping option, Larison Cove, is a canoe-in day-use area on a 1.5-mile-long arm of Hills Creek Reservoir, where motorized boats are prohibited. Two picnic tables and fire rings sit there in a quiet old-growth setting, and dispersed camping is available in the area. A Northwest Forest Pass is required to park at the put-in, which is at FS 2106, after about 3 miles on FS 21. You'll also find a vault toilet and garbage service at the put-in.

Sacandaga Campground

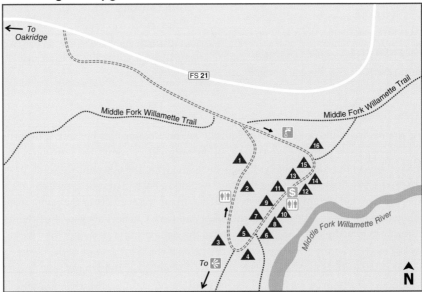

GETTING THERE

From I-5 take Exit 188 or 188A in Eugene, and head east on OR 58. Drive 37.2 miles. Just past Oakridge, turn right onto Hills Creek Road/Kitson Springs Road. Drive 0.5 mile, then turn right onto Forest Service Road 21 (also known as Rigdon Road and Diamond Drive). Drive 24.6 miles to the campground, which will be on the right.

GPS COORDINATES: N43° 29.885'   W122° 20.035'

⛺ Secret Campground

Beauty ★★★★ Privacy ★★★★ Spaciousness ★★★ Quiet ★★★★★ Security ★★ Cleanliness ★★★★

You can practically fish from your tent, and hikers have easy access to the excellent Middle Fork Willamette River Trail.

Who doesn't love stumbling upon a secret campground, and—better yet—discovering that it is as wonderful as that sounds? Well, some secrets are best when shared. This seems doubly true when the name of the secret campground *is* the Secret Campground.

Here's the thing: sometimes nature decides to foil the best-laid plans. The previous edition of this book included a convincingly rapturous description of nearby Timpanogas Campground, which is undoubtedly still an exceptional place to camp—but sadly, wildfire activity made it impossible to reach when we tried to visit for this update. The access road we chose was blocked, and a thick haze of smoke left over from recent fires hung in the air. It happens. Luckily, the campground itself wasn't affected (Eagle Creek Campground in the Columbia River Gorge was not so lucky—we've left it out of this edition, hoping for news that it will soon be rehabilitated), and the odds are good that by the time you read this, Timpanogas will be back on the "yes, definitely visit" list. But in the meantime, at least there's a good alternative nearby.

Hills Creek Reservoir is open to boating, fishing, swimming, and waterskiing.

KEY INFORMATION

CONTACT: American Land & Leisure for Willamette National Forest, Middle Fork Ranger District: 541-782-2283, www.fs.usda.gov/recarea/willamette/recarea/?recid=4513

OPEN: Late May–mid-September

SITES: 6

WHEELCHAIR ACCESS: Not designated

EACH SITE HAS: Picnic table, fire ring with grill

ASSIGNMENT: First come, first served

REGISTRATION: Self-registration on-site

AMENITIES: Vault toilets, no water

PARKING: At campsites; 2 vehicles/site; $7/additional vehicle

FEE: $13

ELEVATION: 1,873'

RESTRICTIONS:

PETS: On leash only

QUIET HOURS: 10 p.m.–6 a.m.

FIRES: In fire rings only

ALCOHOL: Permitted

OTHER: RVs up to 24'; no hookups; maximum 6 people/site; 14-day stay limit; no chain saws

Secret Campground is a little closer to civilization (also known as Oakridge) than Lake Timpanogas, but it still feels like the middle of nowhere—especially if your slightly too-ambitious travel itinerary means that you have to drive into the campground well after dark, because out here, dark means *dark*. Let's say you had your route all perfectly sketched out on a highly detailed topographical map that included every single spidery forest road in the vicinity. But, oops, the one road that connects points A and B is blocked off! If you've done much driving around backwoods Oregon, you know how common this is: maybe it's a downed tree in the road, maybe a washout, maybe (as in our case) a forest fire. Whatever the cause, there's nothing to do but backtrack, grab some coffee, recalibrate, and commit to getting there the long way. And it is kind of a long way from practically anywhere to Oakridge. Then, once you leave the bright lights of Oakridge and turn south on Kitson Springs Road (FS 23), you might as well be driving into a cave. The early part of the route toward Lake Timpanogas hugs one shore of an enormous reservoir, but you'd never know it after sunset. It's no wonder you decide to stop short of your goal and pull in to a campground you've never heard of before: the Secret Campground.

All of which only amplifies the joy of waking up early in the morning surrounded by forest so green and lush it almost looks tropical. Sunlight filters through mossy trees, a river babbles in the background, and, as far as you can tell, there's nary a sign of civilization. This is the stuff!

Each of the six sites has plenty of space and is surrounded by walls of greenery, so it stays nice and quiet. Even better, the campground is well positioned right beside the Middle Fork Willamette River. This means you can practically fish from your tent (be sure to check current regulations with the Oregon Department of Fish and Wildlife first, as specific rules sometimes apply to this part of the river), and hikers have easy access to the excellent Middle Fork Willamette River Trail. This 25-mile one-way trek along the riverbanks links several campgrounds and boat ramps in the area, and it includes parts of the historic Central Military Wagon Road. It's open to mountain bikers and horse traffic as well.

Boaters may want to explore nearby Hills Creek Reservoir, built in 1961 by the U.S. Army Corps of Engineers. The lake is 44 miles around and is open to boating, fishing, swimming, and waterskiing.

From here, it's also very easy to hop onto the Pacific Crest Trail, which passes a few miles east of Timpanogas. And the entire area is laced with tiny forest roads going to obscure trailheads all over the place, so your best bet is to bring along a gazetteer and a picnic and set out for adventure, knowing you have a cozy and comfy place to rest at the end of the day.

Secret Campground

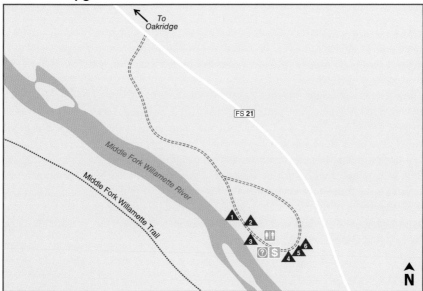

GETTING THERE

From I-5 take Exit 188 or 188A in Eugene, and head east on OR 58. Drive 37.2 miles. Just past Oakridge, turn right onto Hills Creek Road/Kitson Springs Road. Drive 0.5 mile, then turn right onto Forest Service Road 21 (also known as Rigdon Road and Diamond Drive). Drive 18 miles to the campground, which will be on the right.

GPS COORDINATES: N43° 30.951'   W122° 26.596'

36

⚠ Susan Creek Campground

Beauty ★★★★★ Privacy ★★ Spaciousness ★★★ Quiet ★★★ Security ★★★★★ Cleanliness ★★★★

The words North Umpqua evoke sighs, bringing to mind crashing, crystalline waters in a forested canyon, with fish, waterfalls, and magical scenery everywhere.

It's easy to slip into hyperbole when discussing the North Umpqua River. To many Oregonians, and to anglers all over the country, just the words *North Umpqua* evoke sighs, bringing to mind crashing, crystalline waters in a forested canyon, with fish, waterfalls, and magical scenery everywhere.

There are, as one might imagine, campsites all along the Rogue-Umpqua National Scenic Byway, also known in these parts as OR 138. The U.S. Forest Service runs most of these campsites, but Susan Creek is a Bureau of Land Management (BLM) site and is probably the most developed BLM site you'll ever visit. It's a long way from rustic, with landscaped sites, showers, an amphitheater with ranger-led programs, and two hosts for just 29 sites.

Still, it is quite serene, and it is right in the sweet spot of the North Umpqua: too far upstream for the inner-tube crowd, too far downstream for most of the whitewater crowd, right on the banks of the North Umpqua, and shaded by massive Douglas firs. And even though rangers tell us it's full every weekend and most weekdays too, it maintains a quiet, family camping atmosphere.

The swoon-worthy North Umpqua River, near Susan Creek Campground, is a hiker's dream.

KEY INFORMATION

CONTACT: Bureau of Land Management:
541-440-4930, blm.gov/visit
/susan-creek-campground

OPEN: Late April–late October

SITES: 29

WHEELCHAIR ACCESS: Restrooms,
showers, site 19

EACH SITE HAS: Picnic table, fire ring

ASSIGNMENT: 16 sites first come, first
served; 13 sites reservable May 15–
September 15 at 877-444-6777 or
recreation.gov

REGISTRATION: With camp host

AMENITIES: Flush toilets, piped water, showers, amphitheater, horseshoes, river access,
camp hosts

PARKING: At campsites; $5/additional vehicle

FEE: $20; $10 reservation fee

ELEVATION: 940'

RESTRICTIONS:

PETS: On leash only

QUIET HOURS: 10 p.m.–6 a.m.

FIRES: In fire rings only

ALCOHOL: Permitted

OTHER: RVs and trailers up to 25'; no hookups

A dozen of the sites at Susan Creek overlook the emerald-green North Umpqua, where fishing is allowed with flies only. Hiking trails leave both ends of the campground: One heads downstream to a free day-use area and 50-foot Susan Creek Falls, and the other, which is barrier-free, heads upstream to a Watchable Wildlife Site, where you can scan the river for eagles, osprey, or migrating coho or Chinook salmon or sea-run cutthroat trout.

Of course, as nice as the area around Susan Creek is, the larger region it's part of is truly one of the loveliest corners of Oregon. More than 30 miles of the North Umpqua are designated as wild and scenic, and the river is a magnet for outdoor adventurers. Aside from the fishing, floating the river offers everything from Class I and II (novice) to Class IV (dangerous and requiring scouting) rapids. You don't need a permit to float the river, but you do need to know what you're doing, especially above Susan Creek. The BLM web-site for Roseburg (blm.gov/or/districts/roseburg) has a detailed brochure outlining each segment of the river, its challenges and recommended precautions, and peak times when you should avoid floating certain areas to make sure anglers and boaters alike have plenty of river access. No matter your skill level and ambition, start by calling the BLM number listed above or the North Umpqua Ranger Station at 541-496-3532 for up-to-date condi-tions. A quick Internet search will turn up several commercial rafting operations for the bigger-adventure stuff.

And that's just the river! The hiking in this area is also outstanding, highlighted by the 79-mile North Umpqua Trail, which follows the river from Rock Creek (about 10 miles below Susan Creek) to its source at Maidu Lake, high in the Cascades in the shadow of Mount Thielsen, and just a mile from the Pacific Crest Trail. The North Umpqua Trail is divided into 11 segments, broken up by access points, which, in some cases, are also campgrounds or recreation sites on their own. There is an excellent brochure available from the U.S. Forest Service office and website (the North Umpqua District office is on OR 138 in Glide).

One of the great features of the trail is that it's across the river from OR 138; this means that from Susan Creek Campground, the closest access to the trail is about 10 miles downstream at Swiftwater Park or 5 miles upstream at Wright Creek Trailhead. Above Toketee Lake, the trail leaves the highway for good, following the river through a section called the Dread and Terror Segment—named by some folks that got lost up there decades ago. Most hikers consider this the most beautiful part of the trail—it also passes by Umpqua Hot Springs.

As if all this weren't enough, there are shorter trails all over, leading to various meadows, waterfalls, and volcanic features. And OR 138 leads 51 miles up to Diamond Lake (see Thielsen View Campground, page 125, for details) and then another 50 miles to Crater Lake National Park (see Lost Creek Campground, page 104).

So when you're camping at Susan Creek, you're literally surrounded by beauty and adventure. On the other hand, when you're camping at Susan Creek, you might just decide to stay right where you are.

Susan Creek Campground

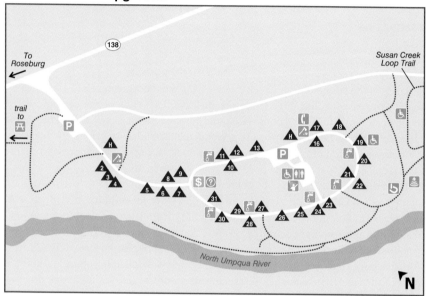

GETTING THERE

From I-5 take Exit 124 in Roseburg (OR 138 E/City Center/Diamond Lake). Turn right onto OR 138 E and drive about 0.5 mile, then turn left onto SE Stephens Street. Drive 0.3 mile, then turn right, back onto OR 138 E. Drive 29.1 miles to the campground on your right.

GPS COORDINATES: N43° 17.800'   W122° 53.600'

37

Thielsen View Campground

Beauty ★★★ Privacy ★★★ Spaciousness ★★★★ Quiet ★★★★ Security ★★★★ Cleanliness ★★

The lone campground on the western shore of Diamond Lake has views galore and a multitude of recreational options.

Thielsen View is one of several U.S. Forest Service campgrounds in the Diamond Lake vicinity, but it's removed from the mayhem of OR 138 because it sits alone on the western shore. Still, with two other campgrounds across scenic Diamond Lake that can accommodate several hundred campers between them, chances are you won't find yourself alone in this seemingly remote territory—although the place clears out substantially around the first of October, so if the weather cooperates, you can sometimes sneak in a last dose of late-season serenity.

Most of the year, though, Diamond Lake is an immensely popular area, particularly with trout anglers who troll the lake's crystalline waters for their share of the plentiful rainbow trout (the lake is stocked with up to 300,000 fingerlings annually). The lake's name comes from the abundance of glassy volcanic rock that litters this region of Umpqua National Forest.

In addition to great fishing, Diamond Lake's popularity can be attributed to a number of other factors. For starters, Diamond Lake is one of the largest natural lakes in Oregon. Add to this its proximity to some spectacular mountain scenery. Follow that up with blissfully warm, dry summer weather. The place is also a convenient distance north of Crater Lake National Park (where, understandably, large numbers of visitors gather in any given summer) and quickly absorbs the overflow. Last but not least, the drive from Roseburg off I-5 follows the pristine and picturesque North Umpqua River most of the way to Diamond Lake on OR 138.

Settle in at the expansive Thielsen View Campground on the shores of busy but beautiful Diamond Lake.

KEY INFORMATION

CONTACT: Umpqua National Forest, Diamond Lake Ranger District: 541-498-2515, www.fs.usda.gov/recarea/umpqua/recarea/?recid=63618

OPEN: Late May–mid-October, depending on snow levels

SITES: 60

WHEELCHAIR ACCESS: Restrooms, sites 17 and 18 in Loop C

EACH SITE HAS: Picnic table, fire ring with grill

ASSIGNMENT: First come, first served; 20 sites reservable at 877-444-6777 or recreation.gov

REGISTRATION: Self-registration on-site

AMENITIES: Vault toilets, piped water, garbage service, boat ramp

PARKING: At campsites; $5/additional vehicle

FEE: $15; $10 reservation fee

ELEVATION: 5,190'

RESTRICTIONS:

PETS: On leash only

QUIET HOURS: 10 p.m.–6 a.m.

FIRES: In fire rings only

ALCOHOL: Permitted

OTHER: RVs up to 24'; no hookups; 14-day stay limit

This stretch of highway has been called one of the prettiest drives in the Western United States in the summertime, and it is also one of the main connectors between western and eastern Oregon. All of these factors add up to plenty of people most of the time.

A sizable share of the wonder at Diamond Lake comes in the form of snowy, knifelike mountain peaks—Mount Bailey to the west and, as the campground name implies, Mount Thielsen to the east. Both will take some time to explore because the only way to fully appreciate them is by foot over arduous trails full of loose, crumbling pumice. (Of course, you'd be forgiven for simply gazing at the peaks from your lakeside campsite, if that's more your scene.) The rock is modern-day evidence of the eruption of Mount Mazama (which formed Crater Lake) some 6,700 years ago.

The upper portion of 9,182-foot Mount Thielsen is a technical climb and should be attempted only by those with the appropriate skills and equipment. Less difficult hikes abound, however, throughout Umpqua National Forest, Mount Thielsen Wilderness, and Oregon Cascades Recreation Area, all within access of Thielsen View Campground. Mount Thielsen Wilderness alone has roughly 125 miles of hiking trails, including a 30-mile section of the Pacific Crest Trail (PCT). Easier trails in the region range from the 3.2-mile ramble to Horse and Teal Lakes (accessed from the South Shore picnic area) to the longer but still gentle Rodney Butte Trail (6.4 miles round-trip). A bit steeper challenge awaits on the Tipsoo Trail, which switchbacks for an elevation gain of 1,500 feet to a spectacular vista, and the Howlock Mountain Trail, which is difficult but connects to the PCT after 7 miles.

Hiking, however, doesn't become an option at the higher elevations much before July, when the heavy snowfalls of winter melt from the trails. In the meantime and at various times throughout the year, there's mountain biking along U.S. Forest Service roads and designated trails (except in wilderness areas). For a full-circle look at the area and to get warmed up to more strenuous activity, try the paved bike paths that circle Diamond Lake. Other options are angling in nearby creeks, hunting, bird-watching, canoeing and kayaking the North Umpqua River, and lowland walks to Lemolo Falls and Toketee Falls. If nothing else, there's sitting in camp and enjoying the incredibly clear mountain air.

The approach of winter doesn't mean a complete end to activity in the Diamond Lake area. Although the campground is closed, the resort on the east shore of the lake is the focal point for a range of skiing and snowmobiling options. At Mount Bailey, you can get in a half dozen exhilarating runs on pristine powder (some say it's the best in the state) via a privately run snowcat system. There's also a Nordic ski center at Diamond Lake Resort, complete with ski rentals and a network of groomed trails. For the snowmobiler there is a plethora of trails, short or long, guided or on your own. You can ride as far as Crater Lake to the south or Crescent Lake to the north (the latter a full-day round-trip of 8 hours).

Thielsen View Campground

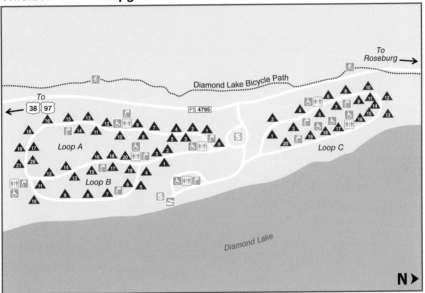

GETTING THERE

From I-5 take Exit 124 in Roseburg (OR 138 E/City Center/Diamond Lake). Turn right onto OR 138/Harvard Avenue and drive about 0.5 mile. Turn left onto SE Stephens Street and drive 0.3 mile. Then turn right onto OR 138 E and drive 78.5 miles. Turn right at the sign for Diamond Lake Recreation Area, and in 0.3 mile turn right onto Diamond Lake Loop/Forest Service Road 4795. Drive 3.2 miles around the north end of Diamond Lake to Thielsen View Campground on the left.

From the intersection of US 97 and OR 140 in Klamath Falls, head north on US 97, and go 59.6 miles. Turn left onto OR 138 W and drive 22 miles. Turn left at the sign for Diamond Lake Recreation Area, and in 0.3 mile turn right onto Diamond Lake Loop/FS 4795. Drive 3.2 miles around the north end of Diamond Lake to Thielsen View Campground on the left.

GPS COORDINATES: N43° 10.169'   W122° 10.081'

EASTERN OREGON

Strawberry Mountain rises above the campground (see page 156).

38

Anthony Lakes Campground

Beauty ★★★★ Privacy ★★★ Spaciousness ★★★★ Quiet ★★★★ Security ★★★★★ Cleanliness ★★★★

The view from just about any campsite at Anthony Lakes is simply picture-perfect.

Anthony Lakes Campground, at 7,100-foot elevation and only 30 miles northwest of Baker City, is part of the Anthony Lakes Recreation Area, which also includes the much smaller and less developed Mud Lake Campground (with only six sites) and the Anthony Lakes Day-Use Area, popular with valley dwellers seeking a high-altitude escape from the heat far below.

The view from just about any campsite at Anthony Lakes is simply picture-perfect, with the shimmering blue of Anthony Lake contrasting against the dark, subalpine forest greens and the rocky, rugged flanks of surrounding Elkhorn Mountains. At this altitude, the fragrances of high-mountain eastern Oregon are irresistible, with pungent notes of woods, earth, and water mingling in the rarefied air. Find one of the sun-warmed, smooth rocks edging the lake, maybe an overhanging tree for a little shade, then dangle a toe or two in the cool waters and indulge yourself.

Unfortunately, if it's a normal summer, the mosquitoes may have you on the go in no time. It's the curse of such a beautiful setting with such a short summer season. They're less of a problem if the snow melts earlier than usual, so it's worth checking ahead. Winter recreationists are in luck because they can enjoy the same views mosquito-free at the Anthony

Anthony Lakes Campground, lovely even under a blanket of snow

KEY INFORMATION

CONTACT: Wallowa-Whitman National
Forest, Whitman Ranger District:
541-894-2393, www.fs.usda.gov/recarea
/wallowa-whitman/recarea/?recid=52199

OPEN: April–October, depending on
snow levels

SITES: 37

WHEELCHAIR ACCESS: Restrooms, 8 sites

EACH SITE HAS: Picnic table, fire ring
with grill

ASSIGNMENT: First come, first served;
reservations for group site only

REGISTRATION: Self-registration on-site

AMENITIES: Vault toilets, drinking water,
boat launch, group shelter, picnic areas,
reservable guard station

PARKING: At campsites or in parking lot for
walk-in sites; $5/additional vehicle ($6 at
RV sites; $10 at overflow parking)

FEE: Tent $10, RV/trailer $14

ELEVATION: 7,100'

RESTRICTIONS:

PETS: On leash only

QUIET HOURS: 10 p.m.–6 a.m.

FIRES: In fire rings only

ALCOHOL: Permitted

OTHER: RVs up to 14'; 14-day stay limit

Lakes Ski Area right next door, along with some of the best powder in Oregon at the highest ski base in the state. Food for thought, if you're so inclined and getting eaten alive.

Campsites come in a variety of options if you arrive early. Despite its out-of-the-way feel, this spot does get busy on summer weekends. The main camping area, configured in two loops, sits above and away from the lake as you drive in off FS 73 (Elkhorn Scenic Drive). These are sites 1–27, and I have to say they would not be my first choice. Very tightly spaced, these sites have decent vegetation ground cover, but privacy is at a premium. Try for one that sits on the outside of the loop for the least-crowded feel.

The best sites, especially for those seeking a bit more privacy, are the walk-ins (28–32), which are in optimum proximity to lake views, generously spaced, and close enough to parking for easy unloading of gear and provisions. They are, however, staggered on either side of the footpath that circumnavigates the lake, which can mean a bit of foot traffic when other campers go out for a shoreside stroll.

Another string of campsites, numbered 33–37, lies on the far south side of the lake beyond the boat launch. These sites are spaced similarly to the walk-in sites, but being on the flats and closer to the lake may enhance the mosquito presence. They are also closer to the boat put-in, which could mean early-morning noise.

Activities abound in the Anthony Lakes area year-round. South and west of the campground is the Baldy Unit of the North Fork John Day Wilderness, a small, rugged area with hiking options in uncrowded terrain. Access to the Elkhorn Range contained within parts of the wilderness is available via the Elkhorn Crest National Recreation Trail, which starts very near Anthony Lakes. Peaks and buttes in the Elkhorns rise as high as 9,100 feet, offering magnificent vistas of this compact but diverse pocket of the Blue Mountains.

You're likely to see as much wildlife as people; the region supports herds of elk and various deer species, black bear, mountain lions, mountain goats, hawks, and the occasional (seasonal) bald eagle. Consequently, however, it's a popular hunting area in the fall. The North Fork John Day River, designated wild and scenic in one stretch west of Anthony Lakes, is known for its abundant fish populations, including Chinook and steelhead migrating in astounding numbers up from the Columbia. Brook trout, Dolly Vardens, and rainbows also thrive in the North Fork.

Historically speaking, more people frequented this area on a regular basis around the turn of the 19th century than do today. The discovery of gold in the late 1860s—combined with a flourishing lumber industry, pioneer ranching, and completion of the transcontinental railroad—contributed to a healthy stretch of boom years for towns such as Granite, Sumpter, Austin, and Bourne. Though much has been destroyed by time, fire, and neglect, a few buildings scattered throughout the region still stand as tribute to that rough-and-tumble period in Oregon history.

One of the best ways to gain a richer appreciation of the area is to drive the entire Elkhorn National Scenic loop—a 106-mile paved route with marked points of interest along the way. It's a good day-tripping option if you make Anthony Lakes Campground your base.

Anthony Lakes Campground

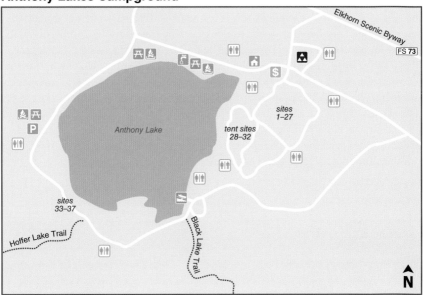

GETTING THERE

Take I-84 to Exit 285 (OR 237/North Powder). Head west on OR 237 S/River Lane. Continue on River Lane 4 miles, then turn left onto Ellis Road. Drive 0.7 mile, then turn right onto Anthony Lakes Highway/Forest Service Road 73/Elkhorn Scenic Byway. Drive 15.4 miles to the campground entrance on the left.

GPS COORDINATES: N44° 57.751'   W118° 13.714'

39

⚕ Buckhorn Campground

Beauty ★★★ Privacy ★★★★★ Spaciousness ★★★★ Quiet ★★★★★ Security ★ Cleanliness ★★

This is the place to pitch your tent, come back to in the evening, tell stories over the crackling campfire, and rub your sore feet after a day of hot, dusty trailblazing.

Buckhorn is a long way from anywhere, not unlike many of the lonely, sacred spots around the Blue Mountains, the Wallowa Valley, and Hells Canyon National Recreation Area. If you're looking for a place to lose yourself, you've found it.

The campground itself is not the centerpiece of the Buckhorn experience; that would be Hells Canyon and the Buckhorn Overlook viewpoint, one of three main lookouts into the canyon. The campground is simply a place to pitch your tent, come back to in the evening, tell stories over the crackling campfire, and rub your sore feet after a day of hot, dusty trailblazing to which you've willingly subjected yourself. OK, so you're not exactly the first person who's been out here (or there wouldn't even be this primitive campground), but at Buckhorn you get the feeling that you could be the last person to visit for a long time.

The sense of loneliness begins on the drive up from Enterprise, when you start out on the Crow Creek Road off of OR 82. At indistinctly marked junctions, the road becomes Zumwalt-Imnaha Road, then Zumwalt-Buckhorn Road, then FS 46. There's no one on the road to ask for directions; ranch houses are tucked deep in the folding fields and usually have gated entrances. When you venture out this way, it's a good idea to carry a detailed map that includes even the smaller gravel roads. (Smartphone-based navigation apps are a fine idea until you lose service—and believe us, you will.)

Hells Canyon Overlook, one of three stunning viewpoints near Buckhorn Campground

KEY INFORMATION

CONTACT: Wallowa-Whitman National Forest, Hells Canyon National Recreation Area: 541-523-6391, www.fs.usda.gov/recarea/wallowa-whitman/recarea/?recid=51823

OPEN: June–late September

SITES: 5

WHEELCHAIR ACCESS: Not designated

EACH SITE HAS: Picnic table; four with fire rings with grill

ASSIGNMENT: First come, first served

REGISTRATION: None

AMENITIES: Pit toilet, no piped water

PARKING: At campsites

FEE: None

ELEVATION: 5,260'

RESTRICTIONS:

PETS: On leash only

QUIET HOURS: None specified

FIRES: In fire rings only

ALCOHOL: Permitted

OTHER: RVs not recommended

All of these anxieties aside, the Zumwalt road ranks as a modern-day magic carpet ride. Miles and miles of burnished gold and brown grasslands roll out before you as you climb gently but steadily on a gravel expressway through this magnificent benchland, the smooth contours and rich colors contrasting sharply with the stark, contorted shadowy jumble of the canyons to the east and the jagged, snowcapped peaks of the Wallowas in the rearview mirror.

The few campsites (five total) that Buckhorn comprises are heavily vegetated (which is a pleasant surprise given the otherwise sparsely shrubbed ground). This is due, in large part, to the presence of Buckhorn Spring, a stalwart little underground spurt that creates an oasis of plant life in this harsh environment. When you drop down to the campground on FS 783 from the main access road (FS 780), which continues on to Buckhorn Lookout, you will feel as though you've stumbled onto a private thicket that could easily be an afternoon resting ground for local deer.

Quickly assessing that *primitive* is a generous word for Buckhorn Campground, you will also recognize that the beauty of this campground lies in its remoteness, its raw simplicity, and its location a mere 100 yards from the mesmerizing view. The familiar "less is more" attitude is a good one to adopt when taking in the wonders from this perch on Oregon's northeastern rim.

By the time you reach the campground, you'll be quite aware that you're near the Buckhorn Overlook. It's less than a mile from the campground, and from there, you actually get two views for the price of one, as the viewpoint sits high above the lower Imnaha River near where it empties into the mighty Snake. Flashes of brilliant sunlight on the river far below catch your eye. Raptors soar in the thermal currents high above. At eye level as far as you can see, ridges and tables and knobs and shelves of varying geophysical proportions and timelines thrust and jut and hunker and lean in an incomparable tableau. It's panorama-plus through a viewfinder, and in all honesty, no photograph can do it justice.

It's easy to see why Chief Joseph and his peaceful band of Nez Perce so loved this land—and why the US government wanted control of it too. Exploitation and misunderstandings ensued, and Chief Joseph was forced out.

Hike to Spain Saddle for continuously impressive views of the Imnaha and Snake River Canyons and even the Salmon River deeper into Idaho. Enjoy Buckhorn for what it once was, for what it is today, and, mostly, for what it isn't. Take away an appreciation of some of the most wild, untamed areas of Oregon desperately trying to remain that way, and whenever it comes time to vote to preserve this special place, do the right thing.

Buckhorn Campground

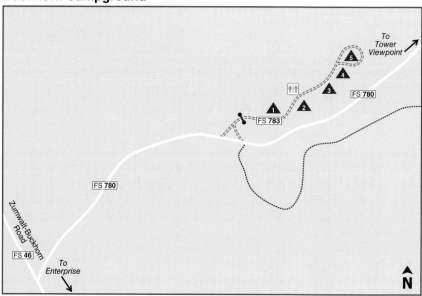

GETTING THERE

From I-84 take Exit 261 in La Grande, and head east on OR 82. Drive 17.7 miles to Elgin. Turn right to stay on OR 82 E and drive 26.6 miles to Wallowa. Turn right to stay on OR 82, and go another 7.6 miles. Turn left to remain on OR 82, and go 10 miles. In Enterprise turn right to follow OR 82. In 3.4 miles turn left (north) onto Crow Creek Road and drive 1.1 miles. Turn right (east) to stay on Crow Creek Road and drive 4 miles. Turn right onto Zumwalt Road and drive 32.6 miles (during which Zumwalt Road becomes Zumwalt-Buckhorn Road and then Forest Service Road 46). Turn right onto FS 780 and drive 0.5 mile to the campground. The roads out here aren't particularly well marked; carry a detailed local map. Nearly the entire drive is on fine gravel, so expect a dust cloud following you in the summer.

GPS COORDINATES: N45° 45.292'   W116° 50.175'

40

Hart Mountain National Antelope Refuge: Hot Springs Campground

Beauty ★★★★★ Privacy ★★★★ Spaciousness ★★★★★ Quiet ★★★★ Security ★★★★★ Cleanliness ★★★★

No place in this book—heck, in Oregon—is more wide open and beautiful than the Hart Mountain National Antelope Refuge.

There's out there, there's really out there, and then there's getting to Hart Mountain National Antelope Refuge from the nearest town of Frenchglen, population 117. You follow OR 205 south about 10 miles, then turn onto a gravel road, often washboarded, that the government says "is not maintained for passenger vehicles," and follow it 37 miles to the headquarters. Sixty-five miles in the opposite direction is Lakeview, a veritable metropolis at 2,321 souls.

In between? A whole lot of wide-open beauty. And antelope. And free creekside campsites with hot springs.

Now, the question in your mind might be, "What's this about 'not maintained for passenger vehicles'?" And you're right to wonder. But in the '93 Sentra Test—can a 1993 Nissan Sentra handle it?—the roads from both Frenchglen and Lakeview did just fine. And while it's longer, the route from Lakeview is better, so plan on taking that route unless you're already in the Frenchglen/Steens Mountain area (like at Page Springs Campground, page 153). Do keep in mind that traveling along these roads will go quite a bit more slowly than you might expect; allow yourself plenty of time.

Immerse yourself in the landscape surrounding Hart Mountain National Antelope Refuge with a dip in the campground's hot springs. *(photographed by Scott Weissbeck)*

KEY INFORMATION

CONTACT: U.S. Fish and Wildlife Service: 541-947-3315, fws.gov/sheldonhartmtn /Hart/management.html

OPEN: Year-round, depending on snow levels; roads can get dicey in winter and spring

SITES: 30

WHEELCHAIR ACCESS: Not designated

EACH SITE HAS: Most have a picnic table

ASSIGNMENT: First come, first served

REGISTRATION: At campground entrance

AMENITIES: A hot spring, pit toilets . . . and not much else

PARKING: At campsites

FEE: None

ELEVATION: 6,000'

RESTRICTIONS:

PETS: On leash only

QUIET HOURS: 10 p.m.–6 a.m.

FIRES: Banned during dry seasons; bring your own wood

ALCOHOL: Permitted

OTHER: RVs and trailers up to 20'

But it's well worth the drive to get here. For starters, have you ever seen antelope? You almost certainly will at Hart Mountain, though it might be from a distance, so bring binoculars or a telescope. Second, no place in this book—heck, in Oregon—is more wide open and beautiful than the Hart Mountain National Antelope Refuge. And yet it's far from being lifeless. Of course, there are the antelope (also known as pronghorn), who are not as shy as you might think; you're likely to have to wait for some to walk across Frenchglen Road, and they might even pose for photos within 100 feet. If you're really lucky, you'll get to see one run; they can go 45 mph, and their eyes work at the equivalent of 8-power binoculars. The refuge website says the eastern area, along Frenchglen Road and Lookout Point, is the best place to spot these stars of the refuge.

And yet it's not all antelope out there; the refuge hosts 239 species of birds, especially on the western edge at the Warner Wetlands, a series of astonishing lakes at the base of amazing cliffs. (Yes, it's the land of superlatives.) The spring migration season is the highlight here, and the refuge has built several blinds for your convenience. Tougher to spot, but still around, are bighorn sheep, bobcats, and coyotes. And there are rattlesnakes, so keep an eye and an ear out, and leash that dog!

In the middle of all this dry vastness, Hot Springs Campground is the place to stay. There are two other campgrounds (one for horses), but Hot Springs is where it's at, with 30 sites stretched along two creeks, most of them tucked into little pockets of aspen trees. It's the very definition of rustic—no water, no fire rings, rough roads, and some sites without tables—but it's also free, and while RVs are allowed, the use of generators is banned. And did we mention the hot springs? There are even three tent-only walk-in sites, but they lack shade and are not in the best part of the campground.

Oh yes, the hot springs! There is one right in the middle of the campground, about 5 feet deep with room for perhaps six adults at a time. The water is not uncomfortably hot, and in 2008 the refuge actually built a stone wall with some benches around it. Some folks grumbled about this because part of the charm before was that you were sitting in the springs with a view of everything. But the flip side of that is that everybody had a view of the springs, and, as you might know, most hot springs in Oregon (including this one) are clothing optional, and most people opt for no clothing. Which is probably why there's now a spiffy, 5-foot stone wall around the springs.

Among the other activities here—that is, other than looking around saying, "Dang!"—your choices include hiking, riding horses, riding (very sturdy) bikes on the roads, rock-hounding (for surface rocks weighing less than 7 pounds), backpacking, and, of course, looking for critters.

After a day spent roaming the high desert, bonding with antelope and migratory birds, and contemplating the vast expanse of blue sky, nothing—not even a little wall around your hot springs—will be able to get between you and a peaceful state of mind.

Hart Mountain National Antelope Refuge: Hot Springs Campground

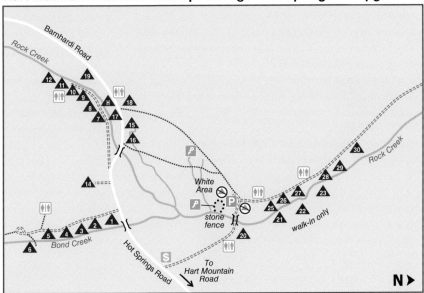

GETTING THERE

From the intersection of US 395 and OR 31 in Valley Falls, head south on US 395 for 17.8 miles. Turn left onto OR 140 E and drive 15.6 miles. Veer left (north) onto Plush Cutoff Road/County Highway 3-13 and drive 18.6 miles to the hamlet of Plush. Continue to the left onto Hogback Road and drive 1 mile, then turn right onto Hart Mountain Road and drive 2 miles. Turn right to stay on Hart Mountain Road and drive 3.5 miles. Turn left to again stay on Hart Mountain Road and drive 17.5 miles. Once in the refuge, follow signs 4.4 miles south to Hot Springs Campground.

GPS COORDINATES: N42° 29.928'   W119° 41.580'

41

⛺ Hidden Campground

Beauty ★★★★★ Privacy ★★★★ Spaciousness ★★★★★ Quiet ★★★★★ Security ★★★ Cleanliness ★★★★

Sun filters through the tall trees and a cooling breeze kicks off the fast-falling Imnaha to make for a heavenly combination.

A peaceful, beautiful, almost poetic setting on the shoulders of the upper Imnaha River, this is one of our favorite little campgrounds in the state. It's even easier to appreciate Hidden Campground after the drive down from Joseph, which is gorgeous but requires a certain degree of alertness, even though it is entirely paved. The road starts off as a gentle grade up on Little Sheep Creek Road, with wide views of the Wallowa Valley as it falls away behind you; as you turn onto FS 39 (also known as the Wallowa Mountain Loop Road), it becomes a twisting, narrow, roller-coaster ride that will either be loads of fun or a bit nerve-racking, depending on your inclinations.

To get here, you'll pass through an area that burned in 1988 and work your way toward the ultimate drop down to the Imnaha River Road (FS 3960), approximately 30 miles from the start of Wallowa Mountain Loop Road (FS 39). Be sure you have a good USGS map of the area, as the road signs can be confusing. (Hint: Start by following signs to Hells Canyon Overlook, then after 30 miles, look for a sign to IMNAHA RIVER CAMPGROUNDS—that's FS 39, and 7 miles later you'll see the Hidden Campground sign to your right, entrance on your left.)

The campground itself is not hidden at all. In fact, it is one of the few campgrounds along the Imnaha that offers gorgeous, open sites with lovely tall grasses under towering ponderosa pines and tamarack. Sun filters through the tall trees and a cooling breeze kicks off the fast-falling Imnaha to make for a heavenly combination on a scorching summer day. Depending on weather, it can also be an absolutely stunning place to see fall colors just before it closes for the season.

Hidden Campground is a gorgeous, not-so-hard-to-find escape along the Imnaha River.

KEY INFORMATION

CONTACT: Wallowa-Whitman National Forest, Hells Canyon National Recreation Area: 541-426-5546, www.fs.usda.gov/recarea /wallowa-whitman/recarea/?recid=51947

OPEN: June–early October

SITES: 10

WHEELCHAIR ACCESS: Vault toilet, 3 sites

EACH SITE HAS: Picnic table, fire ring with grill

ASSIGNMENT: First come, first served

REGISTRATION: Self-registration on-site

AMENITIES: Vault toilets, no piped water

PARKING: At campsites

FEE: $6

ELEVATION: 4,450'

RESTRICTIONS:
PETS: On leash only

QUIET HOURS: None specified

FIRES: In fire rings only

ALCOHOL: Permitted

OTHER: Small RVs or trailers OK; no hookups

Granted, Hidden Campground is about as primitive as they come, with only a picnic table and fire ring with grill at each of its 10 sites. Every site sits well spaced from its neighbors along the river, so there's no chance of a particularly bad spot, and there's plenty of insulating ground cover. Sites 8, 9, and 10 are located on the loop where outgoing traffic circles by and may experience a bit more noise as a result. The wind in the trees and the sounds of the river ought to drown out most disturbances, which would be infrequent anyway. The U.S. Forest Service rates Hidden as a high-use facility, but we've found it barely occupied even in midsummer during the week. Blessedly, there were no RVs, which can be a nuisance at the more developed campgrounds on the way in.

Aside from a few outhouses, there's very little else that interrupts the natural environment. And this is as it should be, as the campground is located within the Hells Canyon National Recreation Area and surrounded by just about every wilderness, wild and scenic, and national forest boundary possible. Immediately west, the officially designated wild and scenic segment of the Imnaha River plunges out of the Wallowa Mountains. A little farther west is the boundary for the Eagle Cap Wilderness and the only trail access into it from this side of the Wallowas (from Indian Crossing Campground at road's end). Due east is Hells Canyon Wilderness and the Wild and Scenic Snake River. Beyond that, there's Idaho. This is the southeasternmost boundary of the Wallowa National Forest, and just across the river on the Imnaha's south bank is the northeasternmost corner of the Whitman National Forest.

If you need any guidance on things to do, a hike into the Eagle Cap Wilderness should be high on the list. Next are the Imnaha River Trail and the Imnaha Crossing Trail. Afterward, make the drive to McGraw Lookout for an unstoppable view over Hells Canyon and some well-placed interpretive plaques and meditation benches. The drive north along the Imnaha River Road leads you to other Hells Canyon overlook points and to the town of Imnaha.

Traveling south along FS 39 and onto OR 86 to the west, the route of the Wallowa Mountain Loop Road continues. This is more than a one-day loop from your starting point at Hidden (unless you get a really early start), so you may want to turn around and retrace your steps near Halfway (the name of the town, not the mileage mark) or take OR 86 east to the town of Copperfield for a different perspective of Hells Canyon and a look at Oxbow Dam.

Paddlers are advised that the Imnaha River in the vicinity of Hidden requires expert skills, and even then it may be a foolhardy venture. The river drops very steeply and is log and debris choked in many spots, demanding a thorough scouting of the waters before you consider any descents. The buddy system is essential in this technical, remote area.

Another option is fishing; the Imnaha is little known to most anglers, but it hosts rainbow and bull trout, as well as wild and hatchery steelhead. Trout season is May 27–October 31; steelhead season on the main stem Imnaha is in spring, winter, and fall.

Hidden Campground

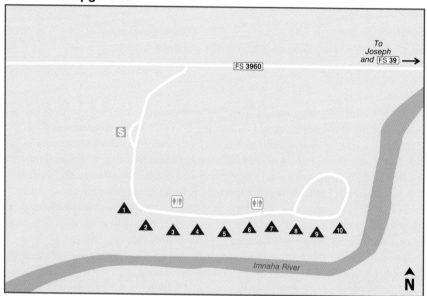

GETTING THERE

From I-84 take Exit 261 in La Grande, and head east on OR 82. Drive 17.7 miles to Elgin. Turn right to stay on OR 82 E and drive 26.6 miles to Wallowa. Turn right to stay on OR 82, and go another 7.6 miles. Turn left to remain on OR 82, and go 10 miles. In Enterprise turn right to follow OR 82. Drive 6.2 miles to the town of Joseph. Turn left (east) onto OR 350/Imnaha Highway and drive 8.1 miles. Turn right (south) onto Forest Service Road 39/Wallowa Mountain Loop and drive 15.6 miles. Turn right onto Coverdale Road and drive 9.2 miles. Turn right onto Upper Imnaha Road/FS 3960 and follow the river about 3 miles to Hidden's entrance on the left. You'll pass a few other campgrounds on the way. The lower Imnaha is home to a daunting system of U.S. Forest Service roads that all seem to look alike, so a good local road map is a must.

Or take I-84 to Exit 302 in Baker City and head east on OR 86. Go 60.2 miles, and turn left onto North Pine Road. In 14.3 miles turn right (south) onto FS 39/Wallowa Mountain Loop and drive 8.8 miles. Turn left onto Upper Imnaha Road/FS 3960, and go 6.9 miles to the campground on the left.

GPS COORDINATES: N45° 06.792'   W116° 58.724'

42

Marster Spring Campground

Beauty ★★★★★ Privacy ★★★★ Spaciousness ★★★★ Quiet ★★★★★ Security ★★★★ Cleanliness ★★★★

The area around Summer Lake is home to wide-open vistas, soaring peaks, and the sprawling wetlands of Summer Lake Wildlife Refuge.

When you think of Oregon's outdoors, do you picture endless swaths of damp forest, covered in moss and ferns and damp six months of the year? If so, you're partly right, but there's much more to it than that. The amount of variety and contrast in this state's ecosystems is extreme, from high desert to coastal rain forest to alpine meadows and everything in between. And Marster Spring Campground is a great base for exploring several of them all at once.

There are two rather amazing ecosystems in this part of Oregon, and Marster Spring Campground sits right between them. That alone would make it worth visiting because you can use it as a base for exploring both the desert and the wetlands around Summer Lake, as well as the high country around Gearhart Mountain Wilderness and Yamsay Mountain.

But it's also true that Marster, on the banks of the Chewaucan River, is a wonderfully pleasant and quiet campground shaded by tall trees. Even better, most people visiting the area zoom right past it, headed uphill or down on Forest Service Road 33. Their loss, your gain.

This part of Oregon gets surprisingly little visitation, and, in fact, many of the campgrounds in the area don't see any real crowds until deer hunting season in the fall. This has

Enjoy long bike rides on the paved roads near Marster Spring Campground and discover scenes such as this. *(photographed by Michael [a.k.a. moik] McCullough/Flickr/CC BY 2.0 [creativecommons.org/licenses/by/2.0])*

KEY INFORMATION

CONTACT: Fremont National Forest, Paisley Ranger District: 541-943-3114, www.fs
.usda.gov/recarea/fremont-winema
/recarea/?recid=59769

OPEN: May 15–October 15 (not maintained October 16–May 14)

SITES: 10

WHEELCHAIR ACCESS: Not designated

EACH SITE HAS: Picnic table, fire ring

ASSIGNMENT: First come, first served

REGISTRATION: At campground entrance

AMENITIES: Vault toilet, water pump, no garbage service

PARKING: At campsites; $2/additional vehicle

FEE: $6

ELEVATION: 4,900'

RESTRICTIONS:

PETS: On leash only

QUIET HOURS: 10 p.m.–6 a.m.

FIRES: In fire rings only

ALCOHOL: Permitted

OTHER: RVs and trailers up to 25'

always seemed odd. The area around Summer Lake is home to wide-open vistas, soaring peaks, and even the sprawling wetlands of Summer Lake Wildlife Area. The spring-fed Ana River nourishes these marshes, which, in March and April, host vast flocks of ducks, geese, and swans, and, in April and May, see more songbirds and other waterfowl. And, by the way, the typical April day in these parts is mostly sunny with a high around 60. Think about that if you live west of the Cascades!

After birding, stop at Summer Lake Hot Springs, less than an hour from camp; there, you can enjoy 103° water in a 15-by-30-foot pool underneath a 1927 bathhouse. (Day use, 8 a.m.–8 p.m., is $10; see summerlakehotsprings.com for more information).

Driving uphill from Marster Spring, you quickly reach the high country, and recreation options abound—mostly hiking and scenic driving. The trail cutting through it all—indeed, stretching some 115 miles across the Fremont–Winema National Forest—is the Fremont National Recreation Trail. This trail (mostly used by horse riders but also open to hikers) traverses such spectacular lookouts as Winter Ridge (2,000' above Summer Lake and 30 miles long!) and 8,196-foot Yamsay Mountain (which offers views from California's Mount Shasta to Oregon's Cascades).

The Fremont Trail also just happens to run right by Marster Spring Campground, across the Chewaucan River, which is said to have pretty decent fishing for rainbow and brook trout. The trail can be accessed at Chewaucan Crossing Trailhead, 0.25 mile south on FS 33, where there's an impressive pedestrian bridge.

Many of the trails here, despite their high elevation, tend to melt out by June, meaning you can usually hike up high here long before you can in the Cascades. But you should also understand that while mosquito season in the Cascades is July, here it's May—and they're incredible, like a living fog. By June they're dying off, the flowers are out in the high meadows, and all is lovely. Grab a map and look for hiking options in Gearhart Mountain Wilderness (22,000 acres, around 7,500' elevation), around Yamsay Mountain, or up on Winter Ridge. Or just drive around, fish, look for beaver ponds and marshes, and enjoy the views.

If you want to camp higher up, there are some nice campgrounds to choose from. Dead Horse Lake and Campbell Lake sit in the hub of a trail network. Smaller and quieter are Lee Thomas and Sandhill Crossing Campgrounds, both on the North Fork of the Wild and Scenic Sprague River around 6,300 feet in elevation.

We recommend either of those if you just want to be up in the mountains in quiet campgrounds. The lakes see more activity, but they also have more options on-site. If you want to be down in the valley, you can even pitch your tent at Summer Lake Hot Springs, although there's no shade there at all.

But if you want to be in the middle of it all, in a nice, quiet campground next to a scenic river, head for Marster Spring.

Marster Spring Campground

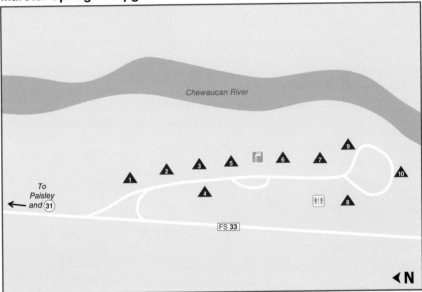

GETTING THERE

From the intersection of US 395 and OR 31 in Valley Falls, drive 22.2 miles north on OR 31 to Paisley. Turn left onto Mill Street/County Highway 2-08 and go 1 mile. Stay left at the Y junction; Mill Street becomes Forest Service Road 33. Drive another 6.1 miles to the campground on the left.

From the intersection of US 20 and US 97 in Bend, head south on US 97, and go 33.6 miles. Turn left onto OR 31, and go 98.2 miles to Paisley. Turn right onto Mill Street/County Highway 2-08 and go 1 mile. Stay left at the Y junction; Mill Street becomes FS 33. Drive another 6.1 miles to the campground on the left.

GPS COORDINATES: N42° 37.463'   W120° 36.336'

43

Minam State Recreation Area Campground

Beauty ★★★ Privacy ★★ Spaciousness ★★★★ Quiet ★★★ Security ★★★★ Cleanliness ★★★★

This is a prime spot if you're bringing a large group along—your group can camp on the large grassy knolls.

If you're looking for a cozy, secluded campsite, look elsewhere: all of the primitive campsites in this campground are in a huge open clearing where you can wave to your neighbors. But don't discount it just yet. What it may lack in privacy, Minam State Recreation Area certainly makes up for in other areas.

For starters, it sits pretty in a remote valley on a steep bank overlooking the whitewater of the Wallowa River, which is a popular destination for both rafters and anglers. Large pine trees dominate the landscape.

American Indians called this area—which extends from the mouth of Indian Valley where the Grande Ronde narrows, down to the confluence of the Grande Ronde and Wallowa Rivers—Hunaha. Lochow, or "lovely little forest," was the central camp for the Nez Perce, who harvested wild vegetables, fruit, fish, and game through the summer months.

Excellent for groups or families traveling together, Minam State Recreation Area offers campsites in a wide-open riverside clearing.

KEY INFORMATION

CONTACT: 541-432-8855, 800-551-6949, oregonstateparks.org

OPEN: April–October

SITES: 22

WHEELCHAIR ACCESS: Vault toilet, 1 site

EACH SITE HAS: Picnic table, fire ring

ASSIGNMENT: First come, first served

REGISTRATION: Self-registration on-site

AMENITIES: Vault toilets, piped water

PARKING: At campsites; $7/additional vehicle

FEE: $10

ELEVATION: 2,500'

RESTRICTIONS:

PETS: On leash only

QUIET HOURS: None specified

FIRES: In fire rings only

ALCOHOL: Permitted at campsites only

OTHER: 14-day stay limit

Two launching points for boaters are located in the nearby day-use area, and you can even rent a raft at the nearby Minam Motel. Some rafters return from their runs with tales of bighorn sheep sightings. Anglers will also enjoy this area, as the river is renowned for steelhead and rainbow trout. You can catch your dinner and make use of that fire ring back at your campsite.

Water adventures aren't the only thing drawing visitors; the nearby Wallowa Mountains offer some of the best all-day hiking and backpacking trails in the state, making this a perfect spot to set up camp along the way and return to after a day of hiking. It's also not nearly as crowded as nearby Wallowa Lake State Park Campground; even on a holiday weekend you're likely to find an empty spot. Keep your eyes open, as the area hosts wildlife such as bear, elk, and deer. On a recent visit, a bear sighting in the campground had been reported just a few days earlier.

While the campsites may seem a little confusing as you first enter the campground—they aren't well marked upon first glance and there's no clear-cut difference between one site and its neighbor—there are advantages to this open type of campground. For one thing, it's a prime spot if you're bringing a large group along because your group can camp on the large grassy knolls. Some of the sites offer asphalt tent pads, and most have water nearby. All of the sites offer views of the Wallowa River. The small store at the nearby Minam Motel will stock you up with ice, food, and fishing supplies, but be warned: It tends to close early, so make sure you don't return from an all-day hiking trip with a big thirst, only to be disappointed. It's best to come prepared, but Elgin is only about 10 miles west, so you're not completely out of luck.

Speaking of Elgin, it's one of those small Oregon towns well worth a visit. There's not all that much to it—the historic town center consists of just a few brick buildings—but it has lots of charm. Don't miss the lovely 1912 Opera House, still in use as a venue for movies, theater, music, and other community events.

If you find yourself recovering from the aches of a long hike or rafting trip, Elgin also offers an unexpected way to view the valley's majestic scenery—by rail. The Eagle Cap Excursion Train (800-323-7330, eaglecaptrainrides.com) offers round-trip rides from nearby Wallowa to Joseph, where you can sit back and enjoy the view from the train's Pullman cars. Don't forget to bring your camera.

However you decide to enjoy this natural setting, keep in mind that the climate in eastern Oregon varies greatly with elevation. The higher up you go, the colder the temperatures and the higher the chance of precipitation. If you're visiting the region during the summer months, be prepared for afternoon thunderstorms and chilly evening temperatures. Don't be surprised if you encounter snow on high country trails at any time of year.

Minam State Recreation Area Campground

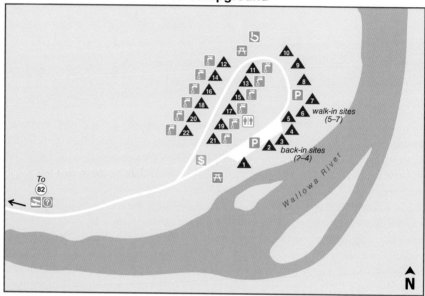

GETTING THERE

From I-84 take Exit 261 in La Grande, and head east on OR 82. Drive 17.7 miles to Elgin. Turn right to stay on OR 82 E and drive 13.2 miles. Turn left (north) at the sign for Minam State Recreation Area. Drive 2 miles to the end of the road and the campground.

GPS COORDINATES: N45° 38.247'   W117° 43.743'

44

North Fork Malheur Campground

Beauty ★★★★★ Privacy ★★★ Spaciousness ★★★★★ Quiet ★★★★ Security ★★★★ Cleanliness ★★★★

The Malheur River starts its 23-mile course in a glaciated valley filled with ponderosa pines, flowery meadows, and big-time views, then flows among old-growth ponderosa pines through a narrow canyon.

Sometimes a campsite is just that: a place where you can camp. That may sound simplistic, but if you were traveling or backpacking, and you were looking for a place to bed down, this is probably what you would want: someplace quiet, out of the way, pretty, in a flat clearing by the side of a lovely river with some fish in it, without many people around, and without any fees.

Well, that's North Fork Malheur Campground: five sites along the banks of a wild and scenic river, with stuff to do all around you, but also a darn fine place to just, well, camp.

And now, a few words of reverence for the North Fork of the Malheur River: When folks talk about the health of a river and an ecosystem, they generally refer to the well-being of some indicator species. On the North Fork of the Malheur, which was designated wild and scenic in 1988, those species are redband trout and especially bull trout.

Are all trout the same? Well, no. A bull trout eats other fish and, as a result, gets really big—up to 2 feet long and 20 pounds. Now, the bull trout is an endangered species because it needs a particular habitat to survive: many miles of cold, clear, oxygenated water (which

The North Fork Malheur Trail begins at this bridge and then follows the river.
(photographed by Musgrove and the Pumi)

KEY INFORMATION

CONTACT: Malheur National Forest, Prairie
   City Ranger District: 541-820-3800,
   www.fs.usda.gov/recarea/malheur
   /recarea/?recid=40132

OPEN: May–October, depending on
   snow levels

SITES: 5

WHEELCHAIR ACCESS: Not designated

EACH SITE HAS: Picnic table, fire ring

ASSIGNMENT: First come, first served

REGISTRATION: None

AMENITIES: Vault toilet, no water

PARKING: At campsites

FEE: None

ELEVATION: 4,700'

RESTRICTIONS:

PETS: On leash only

QUIET HOURS: 10 p.m.–6 a.m.

FIRES: In fire rings only

ALCOHOL: Permitted

OTHER: RVs and trailers up to 25'

we would call bubbly) and a situation the U.S. Forest Service calls minimal historic and current activities. That's a government way of saying "nobody messing with it." Well, the North Fork Malheur is serious Bull Trout Country, as many signs around will remind you. It starts its 23-mile course (all protected as wild and scenic) in a glaciated valley filled with ponderosa pines, flowery meadows, and big-time views, then flows among old-growth ponderosa pines through a narrow, rough canyon with walls as high as 750 feet. Eventually, it joins the Middle Fork Malheur, which is also protected, and together they dance off into the sage and juniper country down below.

And along its scenic way, the North Fork Malheur passes our lovely little campground. And if it's not deer hunting season, you just might have the place to yourself. This is, in part, because the last bit of road (specifically FS 1675, the last 2.4 miles to the campground) is a little rough. You'll see some cattle around, too, but they are kept clear of the campground by cattle guards on the road.

OK, but what if you don't *just* want to camp? Fear not, there are plenty of activities in the surrounding area. A quarter mile down the road you'll find the trailhead for the North Fork Malheur Trail, which follows the river for 12.4 miles; take the footbridge across the river to the trailhead, then follow the trail along the west side of the river. It plunges into a dramatic canyon, which fills up with wildflowers in spring. There are rattlesnakes in the area in warmer weather, so be cautious.

Another thing people love to do in this area is ride mountain bikes, as there are old roads all over the place that are no longer suitable for cars. Bikes are also allowed on the North Fork Trail, and motorized vehicles are not. For any of this, of course, you'd want a really good map of the district, so stop in the Prairie City Ranger District office on the way to the campground. Map in hand, it's possible to create a fun loop ride via Crane Creek Trail and the network of forest roads.

Fishing is allowed; rainbow trout can be kept, but bull trout must be released unharmed.

And if you're wondering about the name Malheur, it literally means "bad hour" in French; the name comes from Peter Skene Ogden, who camped on the river with French Canadian trappers in 1826 and discovered that a cache of furs left there the previous year had been stolen. What he was calling it was the "unfortunate river."

North Fork Malheur Campground

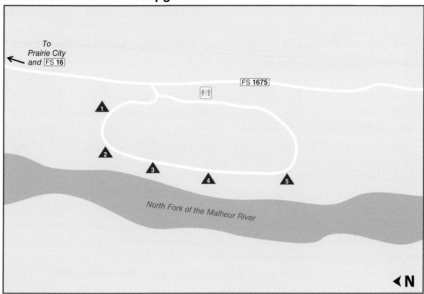

GETTING THERE

From the intersection of US 26 and US 395 in John Day, head west on US 26 for 12.9 miles. In Prairie City, turn right (south) onto South Main Street and drive 0.3 mile. Turn left onto SW Bridge Street, which quickly becomes CR 62/Logan Valley Road. Drive 7.8 miles, then turn left onto Forest Service Road 13 and drive 16.3 miles. At the South Creek Guard Station, turn right onto FS 16 and drive 2.1 miles to a fork. Turn left onto FS 1675 and drive 2.4 bumpy miles to the campground.

GPS COORDINATES: N44° 12.475'   W118° 22.920'

45

⚠ Olive Lake Campground

Beauty ★★★★ Privacy ★★★★ Spaciousness ★★★★★ Quiet ★★★★★ Security ★★★★ Cleanliness ★★★★★

Lodgepole pines, with their slim trunks, provide high-canopy relief from the sun on hot days and precipitation on wet ones.

Olive Lake has played an integral role throughout the history of this region, from the early gold-mining days to its contemporary recognition as a valuable focal point for area recreation, habitat restoration, and historical preservation. The combination makes for an interesting blend, offering opportunities to learn and explore in one of the least-traveled areas of eastern Oregon.

You can reach Olive Lake either by way of OR 7 out of Baker City, or by coming down from the north along US 395 out of Pendleton, or from the west via a more circuitous route off of US 26 near Prairie City. A good map of the state, county, and U.S. Forest Service roads in the lonely outposts of Baker and Grant Counties is a wise traveling accessory if you want to be adventurous yet maintain peace of mind. And whichever way you go, be sure to top up the fuel tank at every opportunity; gas stations are few and far between here, and many of them accept only cash and/or keep extremely limited hours. But it's beautiful country to drive in.

The Olive Lake Campground is shaped like a horseshoe around the north end of the lake, offering either lakefront living or views from just about every site. There are a total of 28 tent sites, 23 of which can also be RV sites. Five sites are walk-in only. There are two group sites and three picnic areas. Sites are gargantuan in size and generously spaced, so

Nearby Fremont Powerhouse also offers cabins for rent.
(courtesy of the U.S. Forest Service–Pacific Northwest Region/public domain)

KEY INFORMATION

CONTACT: Umatilla National Forest, North Fork John Day Ranger District: 541-427-3231, www.fs.usda.gov/recarea/umatilla/recarea/?recid=56605

OPEN: Late May–October (not maintained and no fee November–mid-May)

SITES: 28, 2 group

WHEELCHAIR ACCESS: Restrooms, boat ramp, docks; sites 11, 13, 15, and 16

EACH SITE HAS: Picnic table, fire ring with grill

ASSIGNMENT: First come, first served

REGISTRATION: Self-registration on-site

AMENITIES: Vault toilets, day-use areas, no piped water

PARKING: At campsites and at the boat ramp/dock; 2 vehicles/site; $5/additional vehicle

FEE: $12, no fee November–mid-May

ELEVATION: 6,000'

RESTRICTIONS:

PETS: On leash only

QUIET HOURS: 10 p.m.–6 a.m.

FIRES: In fire rings only

ALCOHOL: Permitted

OTHER: No RV size limit, though not all sites will accommodate large RVs; no hookups; gas and electric boat motors allowed

you won't feel hemmed in. Low-bush undergrowth is spare, which further enhances the feeling of openness. Lodgepole pines, with their slim trunks, don't clutter the campground yet provide high-canopy relief from the sun on hot days and precipitation on wet ones.

Many of the campers who occupied sites on a recent visit had a settled-in look about them, suggesting they had been there a long time. Many of these regulars return year after year to their favorite spots and quickly become part of the scenery. According to the camp hosts, the majority of campers who enjoy Olive Lake are repeat customers.

Olive Lake itself, pitted in its center with an island of trees, sits high in the Greenhorn Range of the Blue Mountains at an elevation of 6,000 feet. The Greenhorn Unit of the North Fork John Day Wilderness can be accessed via a short hike heading southeast from the south end of the lake. The boundary between the Umatilla National Forest and the Malheur National Forest works its way in right angles along high rock buttes and crumbled ridges southwest of the lake. To the north, the largest unit of the North Fork John Day Wilderness encompasses 86,000 acres, creating a protected passageway for the North Fork John Day River and visitors looking to enjoy its wild and scenic designation.

Recreationally, the lake is a destination for anglers, who are allowed to use boats with both electric and gas motors (strange, so close to a wilderness boundary) to chase after their catch. Kokanee, cutthroat, rainbow, and brook trout are the prime fish to catch. A 2.5-mile trail surrounding the lake is an easy evening stroll, but a longer, more challenging hike takes you north and west to Saddle Camp and Ridge. You can hike along the spine of Saddle Ridge or make the crest of Saddle Camp your turnaround point. A loop hike continues down Saddle Ridge and along Lost Creek at various points to return to Olive Lake either via a trail or FS 10. Half of this loop trip winds through designated wilderness where you won't encounter any motorized travel.

Historically, Olive Lake was the water source for the Fremont Powerhouse, which served mining and municipal interests for the first half of the 20th century. A wood-and-steel pipeline was constructed to funnel water nearly straight down the mountainside to the powerhouse. You can still see parts of the pipeline as you travel along FS 10 or along the aforementioned loop hike. The powerhouse has been placed on the National Register of Historic Places and is open to visitors—and its cool steampunk atmosphere and history lesson in 3D make it well worth a peek, if it's open when you arrive. The complex includes a caretaker's house and three other cabins. The cabins have been refurbished and are now available to rent through the U.S. Forest Service.

Olive Lake can be busy in the summer, so it's good to have a nearby alternative in mind.

Olive Lake Campground

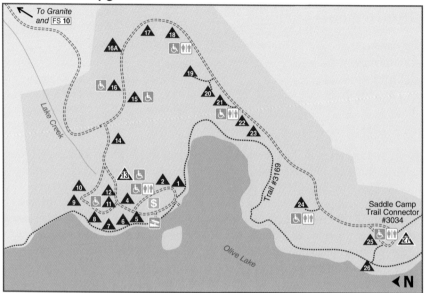

GETTING THERE

From I-84 S near Pendleton, take Exit 209 (US 395 S/John Day/Pendleton). Turn right (south) onto US 395 S and drive 47.4 miles. Turn left onto OR 244 E and drive 1.2 miles. In the center of Ukiah, turn right (south) onto Camas Street, which will become Forest Service Road 52; this is part of the Blue Mountain National Scenic Byway. Drive 49 miles to the town of Granite. Turn right onto FS 10/CR 24 (in about 3.5 miles this paved road will become gravel). Drive 12.1 miles uphill to Olive Lake.

GPS COORDINATES: N44° 47.007'   W118° 35.711'

46

Page Springs Campground

Beauty ★★★★ Privacy ★★★ Spaciousness ★★★ Quiet ★★★★★ Security ★★★★ Cleanliness ★★★★★

When was the last time you had an opportunity to drive to the top of a 9,773-foot mountain that unabashedly bares so many of its geologic secrets?

One look at the southeastern expanse of Oregon, roughly 60 miles south of Burns, and you know you're in a place where country-western music is as common as corn bread. Mile after dusty mile, scraggly sagebrush, twisted juniper, and jagged rimrock share a landscape punctuated only by the hulk of mile-high Steens Mountain. This is the highest fault-block mountain in the nation and a snowcapped beacon for all of southeast Oregon.

The region was once the turf of the largest cattle ranch in the United States. Pete French arrived in the Donner und Blitzen River Valley in 1872 with 120 head of cattle and built an empire that totaled 45,000 cattle and 200,000 acres. Cattle operations still exist in parts of the Steens Mountain area today. But with all the natural wonders to behold, outdoor recreation and tourism are emerging as alternatives to traditional sources of income, which are gradually fading away.

Page Springs Campground sits invitingly in the midst of this spectrum. Maintained by the Bureau of Land Management (BLM) out of its Burns District office, Page Springs is one of three public campgrounds that the bureau provides for visitors. It is centrally located for interesting day trips, which await in just about every direction. It's also the only one of the three campgrounds that is open all year. (Steens Loop Road closes during winter, but the campground sits just outside the gate.)

The Donner und Blitzen River and Steens Mountain flank Page Springs Campground.
(courtesy of Bureau of Land Management Oregon and Washington/Flickr/CC BY 2.0 [creativecommons.org/licenses/by/2.0])

KEY INFORMATION

CONTACT: Bureau of Land Management:
541-573-4400, blm.gov/visit
/page-springs-campground

OPEN: Year-round; host available
May–September

SITES: 34

WHEELCHAIR ACCESS: Not designated

EACH SITE HAS: Picnic table, fire ring
with grill

ASSIGNMENT: First come, first served

REGISTRATION: Self-registration on-site

AMENITIES: Pit toilets, piped water, garbage
service, group picnic shelter

PARKING: At campsites

FEE: $8

ELEVATION: 4,200'

RESTRICTIONS:

PETS: On leash only

QUIET HOURS: 10 p.m.–6 a.m.

FIRES: In fire rings only

ALCOHOL: Prohibited

OTHER: No hookups for RVs; no stock trailers

Once you've settled in among the sagebrush and aspens, stretch your legs after the hot, dusty drive and explore the immediate surroundings on a 1.8-mile stroll that follows the meandering Donner und Blitzen River through tall stands of surprisingly lush grasses and other hardy indigenous vegetation. This short path is part of a longer route known as the 750-mile Oregon Desert Trail, a still-in-progress initiative to connect some of the state's wildest arid regions.

Now that you're warmed up (or cooled down, more accurately), consider the more distant options. If you're visiting the area in summer, you may want to escape the intense, merciless heat with a drive around Steens Mountain National Backcountry Byway. Be sure to fill your gas tank and carry extra water for both you and the car. Plan to carry at least a gallon per person per day—although that doesn't seem quite adequate around here, especially if you're hiking. Better to carry too much than too little. The road to Steens is quite rough, the entire loop distance is 66 miles, and what minimal emergency services exist are in Frenchglen, which will be well behind you once you set out. The weather can change quickly and dramatically, so be prepared for extremes of wind and precipitation. Snow is not uncommon in midsummer at higher altitudes. One last thing: The road is not recommended for RVs.

While all this emergency preparedness may sound either overly dramatic or a bit daunting, you'll be thankful later. Once you reach the summit of Steens, you'll want to stick around a while and take in all that this magnificently desolate area has to offer. And you'll make numerous stops along the way, as there are overlooks and short hikes aplenty to distract you.

Take your time and enjoy the journey. Think about it: When was the last time you had an opportunity to drive to the top of a 9,773-foot mountain that unabashedly bares so many of its geologic secrets? Witness the effects of glacial activity with such clear-cut examples as Kiger, Little Blitzen, Big Indian, and Wildhorse Gorges—massive U-shaped troughs up to 0.5 mile deep. The mountain is a veritable living laboratory for botanists and biologists, with five distinct habitat zones ringing its slopes.

Wildlife abounds in the Steens Mountain area, and Malheur National Wildlife Refuge just north of Page Springs provides viewing areas from which as many as 280 species of birds and nearly 60 species of mammals have been observed. The refuge's 185,000 acres of lakes, ponds, marshes, and soggy meadows rank it as one of the top havens for breeding waterfowl, upland game birds, fur-bearers, and big game. Because Page Springs is open all year, bird enthusiasts should try to plan their trips to the refuge anytime late February–May, when wave after wave of migratory winged creatures take to the skies: tundra swans, Canada geese, lesser sandhill cranes in February; shorebirds such as willets, long-billed curlews, and avocets in April; and thousands upon thousands of songbirds in May. Beware, however, of the heavy mosquito population present until midsummer. Herds of the wild Kiger mustang, a direct descendant of the horse introduced to America by Spanish conquistadors, still roam areas around the Steens and are managed by the BLM. A wild horse and burro adoption program is a popular and humane means through which the Burns BLM controls the size of these herds.

Page Springs Campground

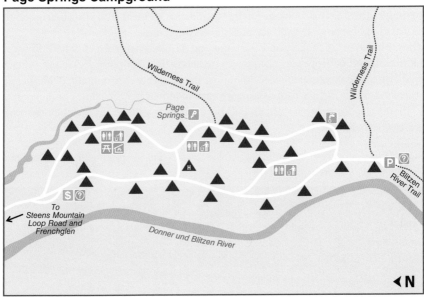

GETTING THERE

From the intersection of US 20 and US 395 in Burns, head west on US 20/US 395 for 2.8 miles. Turn left (east) onto East Monroe Street/OR 78 E and drive 1.6 miles. Turn right (south) onto OR 205 and drive 58.3 miles to the town of Frenchglen (named in honor of cattle baron Pete French and his equally ambitious father-in-law, Hugh Glenn). Veer left onto Steens Mountain Loop, and drive about 3.2 miles. The campground is adjacent to the oasis-like Donner und Blitzen River.

GPS COORDINATES: N42° 48.358'   W118° 52.060'

47

Strawberry Campground

Beauty ★★★★ Privacy ★★★★ Spaciousness ★★★★ Quiet ★★★★★ Security ★★★ Cleanliness ★★★

A cool haven in Malheur National Forest high above the valley floor.

Summer travel in and around the historic burgs of Prairie City, John Day, Mount Vernon, and Dayville is marked by intensely hot days that can sap the strength and resolve of even the hardiest road warrior. If you are about to reach the wilting stage when passing through Prairie City, turn south onto Bridge Street, cross the John Day River, and follow Strawberry Road to its end. Your reward is a cool haven in Malheur National Forest high above the valley floor.

According to a great book called *Oregon Geographical Names*, some of the original settlers named Strawberry Mountain for the abundance of local wild strawberries, and the name just kind of spread to, well, darn near everything else.

Thus, Strawberry Campground is at the end of Strawberry Road, where Strawberry Creek rumbles off of Strawberry Mountain, which is the high point (9,038') of the Strawberry Range and constitutes the focal point of the Strawberry Mountain Wilderness. Oh, yes, there's Strawberry Lake too. At least it's easy to remember the names of things around here. There's also Strawberry Falls, and it's probably only a matter of time before someone dubs Strawberry Spring.

Strawberry Lake Trail climbs 700 feet as it leaves the campground and heads to the lake through shaded wilderness. *(photographed by Erich Rebenstorf)*

KEY INFORMATION

CONTACT: Malheur National Forest, Prairie
City Ranger District: 541-820-3800,
www.fs.usda.gov/recarea/malheur
/recarea/?recid=40164

OPEN: Late May–October

SITES: 10

WHEELCHAIR ACCESS: Not designated

EACH SITE HAS: Picnic table, fire ring
with grill

ASSIGNMENT: First come, first served

REGISTRATION: Self-registration on-site

AMENITIES: Vault toilets, piped water

PARKING: At campsites; $4/additional vehicle

FEE: $8

ELEVATION: 5,700'

RESTRICTIONS:
PETS: On leash only

QUIET HOURS: 10 p.m.–6 a.m.

FIRES: In fire rings only

ALCOHOL: Permitted

OTHER: RVs and trailers not recommended;
no hookups

The drive up to the campground rises gradually through the grassy meadows of private ranchlands and then turns immediately uphill for a gutsy, gravelly climb in the last few miles. As you enter the campground, cross Strawberry Creek to find yourself in a pleasant little forested park hugging the hillside.

The campground is shaped in a near-perfect circle and follows the natural contours of the hillside, with some sites on higher ground, some recessed from the camp road, and some nestled in little glens. It's hard to say which are the better sites, as most are visible to each other; the sites on the outer arc of the circle probably afford the most privacy.

Strawberry Campground is a logical base for some good hiking in the Strawberry Mountain Wilderness, but the elevation gains coming in from the north can be abrupt. A popular route is the Strawberry Basin Trail, which leads to a vista below the summit of Strawberry Mountain. The rise is moderate and the one-way mileage is just over 5 miles, with stops at Strawberry Lake and Strawberry Falls at roughly the 1- and 2-mile marks, respectively. These make for good short outbound destinations to test the limbs and get the muscles warmed.

Other hiking options await in the Aldrich Mountains to the west and at Lookout Mountain to the east. Access to these two areas requires driving part (or all, if time allows) of the scenic loop that encircles the compact Strawberry Mountain Wilderness. The route is an easy 75 miles, linking two state highways, U.S. Forest Service roads, and a county road—paved the entire way—for a 360-degree view of Grant County's tallest peak and the surrounding environs. Some of the easiest hiking access to Strawberry Mountain's summit is from the south up through Logan Valley. Forest Service Road 1640 takes you to trailheads that begin deep in a narrow notch between wilderness boundaries, thus putting you within a reasonably short and gradual ascent to the top.

While the pioneers who first made their way into the Upper John Day Basin are long gone, a proud heritage is strongly evident today in the number of historical societies, museums, and markers that preserve the area's colorful past, shaped mainly by the gold mining, ranching, lumbering, and transportation industries. If you're interested in the human activities that shaped the many fascinating regions of Oregon, it's worth taking time to visit places such as the Kam Wah Chung & Co. Museum in John Day or the DeWitt Museum in Prairie City. There's a lot to learn from the artifacts, memorabilia, and photographs on display.

For a taste of a real working ranch, stop in at Oxbow Ranch on Strawberry Road. The 7,000-square-foot remodeled ranch house operates as a bed-and-breakfast with beautifully appointed guest rooms. For guests of the ranch or out-of-towners passing through, trail-riding and carriage tours are also available (for a fee).

Strawberry Campground

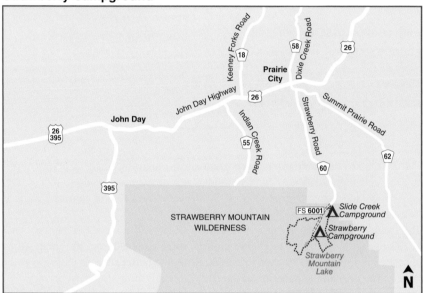

GETTING THERE

From the intersection of US 26 and US 395 in John Day, head west on US 26 for 12.9 miles. In Prairie City, turn right (south) onto South Main Street and drive 0.3 mile. Turn left onto SW Bridge Street, and then in just a few hundred feet turn right onto Bridge Street (which will then quickly become Strawberry Road). Drive 11 miles to the campground at the road's end. The last several miles climb very steeply and are not recommended for trailers or RVs.

GPS COORDINATES: N44° 19.196'   W118° 40.518'

48

Two Pan Campground

Beauty ★★★★★ Privacy ★★★★ Spaciousness ★★★★ Quiet ★★★★★ Security ★★★ Cleanliness ★★★★★

Tucked away in a thickly wooded area at the intersection of road's end and trail's start, this base camp is ideal for exploring the magical Eagle Cap Wilderness.

In the far northeastern corner of Oregon on a broad, grassy plain that once was the beloved homeland of the proud Nez Perce sits a magical little kingdom of imposing granite peaks, flower-choked meadows, rushing glacial creeks, and crystalline alpine air.

Eagle Cap Wilderness, rising high above the Wallowa Valley in the Wallowa Mountains, is regularly referred to as Little Switzerland and even sports a Matterhorn of its own. The American version of this mountain, which is in a different drainage from Two Pan Campground, is the second-highest peak in the Wallowas at 9,826 feet; the highest peak is Sacajawea at 9,832 feet.

Following close on their heels are several dozen other peaks above 8,000 feet. In fact, Oregon has 29 peaks that are 9,000 feet or higher. Seventeen of them are clustered in Eagle Cap, the largest wilderness tract in Oregon at more than 350,000 acres.

One of the higher peaks (Eagle Cap, at 9,595') is accessed by a hiking trail right out of Two Pan; the trail leads hikers to the top, so consider picking up a trail map and going for it.

Two Pan makes an ideal base camp for some of the area's best hiking trails.

KEY INFORMATION

CONTACT: Wallowa-Whitman National Forest, Eagle Cap Ranger District: 541-426-5546, www.fs.usda.gov/recarea/wallowa-whitman/recarea/?recid=51597

OPEN: Mid-June–November

SITES: 5

WHEELCHAIR ACCESS: Not designated

EACH SITE HAS: Picnic table, fire ring with grill

ASSIGNMENT: First come, first served

REGISTRATION: Self-registration on-site

AMENITIES: Vault toilets, no piped water; stock watering tank and hitch rack

PARKING: Parking lot in campground

FEE: $5

ELEVATION: 5,600'

RESTRICTIONS:

PETS: On leash only

QUIET HOURS: None specified

FIRES: In fire rings only

ALCOHOL: Permitted

OTHER: No RV or trailer accommodations; Wilderness Visitor Permit required (self-issued at trailhead, no fee)

Two Pan Campground itself is tucked away in a thickly wooded area at the intersection of road's end and trail's start, which makes it an ideal base camp for exploring the aforementioned magic kingdom. It's a tiny little campground, with just a few sites hidden among the trees.

The dirt road to Two Pan is also a treat; narrow and a bit rough in places, it follows the Wild and Scenic Lostine River and offers many views of the riverside beauty that is perhaps less evident at Two Pan, piercing deep into the Wallowa range and gaining altitude steadily once it enters the canyon. The drive up from the valley floor and into the canyon is an education in both the geology and history of the area. About a million years ago, a large glacier carved out the Lostine River Canyon as it advanced down from the center of the Wallowa Mountains. Grass-covered mounds in the lowlands, known as moraines, are rock and soil deposits left by the glacier in its advance-and-melt periods over hundreds of years. Based on the height of the moraines, geologists estimate that ice as thick as 400 feet once covered this area.

Pole Bridge Picnic Area (a bit past the national forest boundary along the river road) is the site of an old bridge, constructed entirely of poles, that once crossed the river here. About all that's left is a piece of foundation, but it's a nice excuse to stop. Fortify yourself for the remainder of the drive with a snack as you examine further evidence of glacial activity in the deep gorge that the river has cut into the canyon. This is about 0.5 mile up the road from the picnic grounds.

Two miles farther is an even better opportunity to view the natural beauty of the Wild and Scenic Lostine River. A short trail takes you to an overlook of Lostine Gorge, a dramatic plunge between steep canyon walls where vegetation works hard to survive amid the predominant rocks and boulders.

The Wallowa Mountains were once the site of busy gold and silver mining. The ramshackle remains of cabins and outbuildings on the privately held Lapover Ranch (at mile 16) are all that's left of mining claims established by settlers from Kansas in 1911. They got in just under the wire—the Wallowa National Forest received its federal designation later that same year. Until Lostine Road was completed to its current end at Two Pan in 1955, the canyon was a popular route for sheepherders moving their flocks to and from the alpine meadows. Apparently, that is how Two Pan got its name: at some point in all their comings and goings, sheepherders passing through left two frying pans hanging from a tree. OK, it's not the juiciest story, but facts are facts!

When out sightseeing, you'll be tempted to drink straight from the cold, gushing Lostine to quench your thirst. Hold that thought, and keep in mind that the Eagle Cap Wilderness is full of mountain goats, bighorn sheep, elk, deer, and a variety of smaller wild animals. This dramatically increases the risk of giardiasis (which causes diarrhea). It's always wise to boil, treat, or filter the glacial flow, unfortunate as that may seem.

If you want seclusion on your exploration of Eagle Cap Wilderness, avoid the Lakes Basin region, which gets overrun by the crowds from Wallowa Lake. If you want to avoid the mosquitoes and biting flies (which are as thick as the crowds in midsummer), go in September. Either way, you'll need a Northwest Forest Pass or (self-issued) Wilderness Visitor Permit to park at the trailhead. If you want to treat yourself after roughing it in the wilds, stop in at Wallowa Lake Lodge (on the south shore at the end of OR 82). This fine old resort offers pleasant rooms, fine dining, and lively banter with the friendly staff.

Two Pan Campground

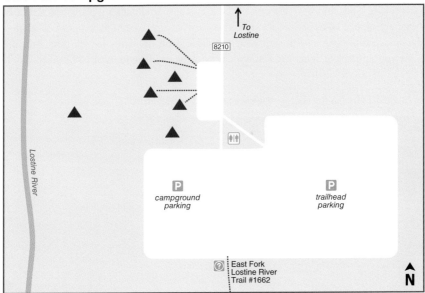

GETTING THERE

From the intersection of OR 3 and OR 82 in Enterprise, drive west on OR 82 for 10 miles to Lostine. Turn left onto Lostine River Road/Forest Service Road 8250 and drive 18 miles, all the way to its end at the campground. The road is paved for the first 7 miles out of town.

GPS COORDINATES: N45° 15.011'   W117° 22.593'

49

Wallowa Lake State Park Campground

Beauty ★★★★★ Privacy ★★ Spaciousness ★★★ Quiet ★★ Security ★★★ Cleanliness ★★★

Bring your camera along to snap shots of the sparkling lake surrounded by the snow-capped mountain peaks.

This is the big tamale of Oregon campgrounds. It's not really the campground itself that is noteworthy, but its impressive neighbors set Wallowa Lake State Park apart and make this area a must-visit place. The campground is, in fact, on the large and busy side, but the facilities are great, with something for just about anyone, whether you're staying for a week and need to do some laundry, bringing along a pet, craving a hot shower, or just want to splurge and glamp it up in a yurt.

For starters, Wallowa Lake is popular for boating and fishing. Word to the wise: Bring your camera along to snap shots of the sparkling lake surrounded by the snowcapped mountain peaks.

The Wallowa (pronounced "wa-LA-wa") area is also renowned as the entrance point for popular hiking trails and perhaps one of the area's best backpacking trails: the Lakes Basin Trail, where alpine lakes reflect an up-close view of the 10,000-foot peaks of Eagle Cap Wilderness. Simply gazing through your windshield on the drive in will take your breath away, as you encounter what are known as the Alps of Oregon. Not to be outdone, Hells

Many Oregonians have a soft spot for Wallowa Lake and its recreationally blessed surroundings.

KEY INFORMATION

CONTACT: 541-432-4185, 800-452-5687, oregonstateparks.org

OPEN: Year-round

SITES: 88

WHEELCHAIR ACCESS: Restrooms, showers, day-use area; yurts 18 and 19; sites A9 and A11 (51 and 73)

EACH SITE HAS: Picnic table, fire ring

ASSIGNMENT: First come, first served, or by reservation at 800-452-5687 or reserveamerica.com

REGISTRATION: At campground entrance

AMENITIES: Flush toilets, hot showers, laundry, firewood

PARKING: At park entrance and at campsites; $7/additional vehicle

FEE: $20; $8 reservation fee

ELEVATION: 4,450'

RESTRICTIONS:

PETS: On leash only

QUIET HOURS: 10 p.m.–6 a.m.

FIRES: In fire rings only

ALCOHOL: Permitted at campsites only

OTHER: RVs and trailers allowed

Canyon on the Oregon–Idaho border—a short 30-minute drive away—is the deepest gorge in North America, at 1 mile, and is a popular whitewater-rafting destination.

But you don't need to travel far to see any action. It seems like everything you could possibly want is in this area (including a wedding chapel!). Guided horseback tours, canoeing, restaurants, even bumper cars, and a minigolf course are among the offerings.

You can also ride a tramway to the top of 8,200-foot Mount Howard, with views of Wallowa Lake and the Eagle Cap Wilderness. Board the tram at quaint Wallowa Lake Village, a town designed to resemble those you might ramble through in the Swiss Alps (it bills itself as The Switzerland of America).

The little town of Joseph nearby is worth a trip too, with local artists' galleries and shops lining the main drag. In a world of overdeveloped mountain towns, Joseph is a refreshing blend of modernity that still manages to maintain its authenticity. All of this means one thing, though: it can get packed, especially on a holiday weekend. (Trust me, you shouldn't even think about showing up without reservations in hand on a long summer weekend, unless you want the campground entrance staff to snicker at you.)

Besides the campground's 88 tent-only sites, the park offers 121 full-hookup sites, two wooden yurts, and one deluxe two-story cabin, plus a hiker-biker area. The facilities throughout the campground are top of the line.

Bird-watching enthusiasts enjoy Wallowa Lake State Park for the abundance of feathered species that enjoy this lovely land, including pheasants, quail, hummingbirds, and the rarely spotted belted kingfisher. Some of the better birding areas near the park include the Chief Joseph Mountain Trail and Old Chief Joseph's grave site.

Guided hunting trips are also popular here; those with the proper permits can pull in big game such as elk, bears, cougars, and even bighorn sheep.

The park offers two picnic areas, a marina, and a boat launch. For those in the mood to test the water but not necessarily looking to plunge in, try parasailing, offered May–September. Purchase tickets at the Eagle Cap Wilderness Adventures & Pack Station.

The Wallowa Lake Highway Forest State Scenic Corridor, a day-use site located along the Wallowa River, is a popular fishing and wildlife-viewing area. Steelhead fishing is popular during the spring and fall. The canyon rises steeply on both sides of the road, and you might see the deer, elk, and bears that live here. Flowers blanket the area in the spring.

If you come at the end of September, you'll enjoy joining the locals at the town's annual Alpenfest fair, a Swiss-Bavarian festival that has been staged in the traditional Oktoberfest style every autumn since 1974.

If you're looking for a place to bring a group with varied interests—and particularly if you can manage to get away when it's not one of the summer holiday weekends—you can't go wrong with this fascinating area.

Wallowa Lake State Park Campground

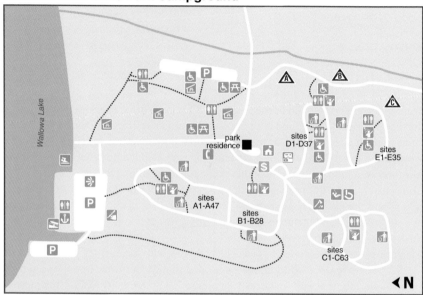

GETTING THERE

From the intersection of OR 3 and OR 82 in Enterprise, drive south on OR 82 E for 6.4 miles to Joseph. Continue onto OR 351 S and drive 5.9 miles. Turn right onto Marina Lane and continue straight to the campground on the left.

GPS COORDINATES: N45° 16.858'   W117° 12.767'

50

Williamson Campground

Beauty ★★★★ Privacy ★★★★ Spaciousness ★★★★ Quiet ★★★ Security ★★★ Cleanliness ★★★★

Eagle Cap is home to some of the best hiking and backpacking in the state, with forested trails leading to brilliant alpine lakes and lush green valleys carved by glaciers eons ago.

Are you a lake person or a river person? Not that you have to choose, of course—but most campers seem to have a preference. If rivers are your thing, you could do worse than spending a night or two at tiny Williamson Campground, with five tent-only sites perched right along the bank of the lovely Lostine River.

The Wild and Scenic Lostine River, designated in 1988, originates at Minam Lake in the Eagle Cap Wilderness and carves its way lazily through a beautiful forested canyon, with plenty of campgrounds, fishing holes, and Instagram-worthy scenic photo spots along the way. As a bonus, it has the advantage of being pretty easy to get to, given the mostly paved (up to the wilderness boundary when it fades to gravel) and very scenic Lostine River Road that runs alongside the bank of the river.

At Williamson Campground, enjoy spacious sites perched beside the Wild and Scenic Lostine River.

KEY INFORMATION

CONTACT: Wallowa-Whitman National Forest, Wallowa Mountains Ranger District: 541-523-6391, www.fs.usda.gov/recarea /wallowa-whitman/recarea/?recid=51611

OPEN: June–early October

SITES: 13 (5 are tent-only)

WHEELCHAIR ACCESS: Not designated

EACH SITE HAS: Picnic table, fire ring with grill

ASSIGNMENT: First come, first served

REGISTRATION: Self-registration on-site

AMENITIES: Vault toilets, no water

PARKING: At campsites

FEE: $6

ELEVATION: 4,900'

RESTRICTIONS:

PETS: On leash only

QUIET HOURS: None specified

FIRES: In fire rings only

ALCOHOL: Permitted

The campground puts you within easy striking range of the popular Eagle Cap and all its outdoor pursuits. It's also just a few miles from the (very small) campground at Two Pan Trailhead (see page 159), making Williamson a reasonable alternative if Two Pan is full or if you don't quite feel up to driving the last bit of rough road the night before a long hike. On summer weekends and holidays, this area gets extremely busy, and for good reason: Eagle Cap is home to some of the best hiking and backpacking in the state, with forested trails leading to brilliant alpine lakes and lush green valleys carved by glaciers eons ago. Anglers flock to the rivers and lakes here, and it's a popular area for horseback riding and camping. Bottom line: It's worth doing whatever scheduling gymnastics you need to do to get here outside of the peak season, when you're much more likely to have all this natural splendor to yourself. (The downside is that the season can be pretty short; snow doesn't start to melt along the hiking trails until July, and it's usually back as early as October. But if you have the right cold-weather gear, early fall is a spectacular time to visit this area.)

Note that all visitors to the Eagle Cap Wilderness area need to carry a Wilderness Visitor Permit (one per group). These are free and self-issued at each trailhead.

For hikers and backpackers, the Lostine trail loop to Minam and Mirror Lakes is a must. It's basically a showcase of all the area's highlights: those awesome U-shaped valleys, craggy peaks, thick wooded areas, rivers, lakes, and tons of wildlife, including bighorn sheep, pica, elk, and white-tailed deer. This should be obvious, but bring a good camera! The trailhead is at Two Pan, where there's a decent-size parking lot, as well as the aforementioned campground. It's wise to check the weather forecast and current road conditions before setting out, especially early or late in the season.

If you happen to drive out from Portland, getting here takes about 6 hours, so it's nice to have a few options for camping the night before you set out the trail. Then again, if you manage to snag one of those riverside campsites along the river at Williamson, you might just be perfectly content to stay put. Day-hikes are plentiful in the surrounding wilderness, and you're only 30 miles from Wallowa Lake State Park, as well as the fun little towns of Enterprise and Joseph. Or you could just hang out by the river.

In short, Williamson makes a great base camp, whether your ambitions for exploring the surrounding area include epic hikes or are more along the lines of walking back to the car to grab a sandwich and maybe taking a scenic drive.

Near the entrance to the campground you'll find a small interpretive site with information about the trout and salmon that populate the river. A gravel road makes the short loop of the campsites; the five tent sites are closest to the river, set at slightly different elevations, which adds a bit of privacy and seclusion.

Williamson Campground

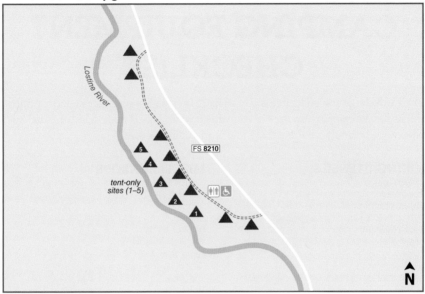

GETTING THERE

From the intersection of OR 3 and OR 82 in Enterprise, drive west on OR 82 for 10 miles to Lostine. Turn left onto Lostine River Road, which becomes Forest Service Road 8210, and drive 11.1 miles to the campground on the right. The road is paved for the first 7 miles out of town.

GPS COORDINATES: N45° 20.535'   W117° 24.697'

APPENDIX A

CAMPING EQUIPMENT CHECKLIST

Except for the large and bulky items on this list, I keep a plastic storage container full of the essentials for car camping, so they're ready to go when I am. I make a last-minute check of the inventory, resupply anything that's low or missing, and away I go.

COOKING UTENSILS
Aluminum foil
Bottle opener
Bottles of salt, pepper, spices, sugar, cooking oil, and maple syrup in waterproof, spill-proof containers
Can opener
Corkscrew
Cups (plastic or tin)
Dish soap (biodegradable), sponge, and towel
Fire starter
Flatware
Food of your choice
Frying pan, spatula
Fuel for stove
Lighter, matches in waterproof container
Plates
Pocketknife
Pot with lid
Stove
Wooden spoon

FIRST AID KIT
See page 3.

SLEEP GEAR
Pillow
Sleeping bag
Sleeping pad, inflatable or insulated
Tent with ground tarp and rainfly

MISCELLANEOUS
Bath soap (biodegradable), washcloth, and towel
Camp chair
Candles
Cooler
Deck of cards
Flashlight/headlamp
Paper towels
Plastic zip-top bags
Sunglasses
Toilet paper
Water bottle
Wool blanket

OPTIONAL
Barbecue grill
Binoculars
Field guides on birds, plants, and wildlife identification
Fishing rod and tackle
Lantern
Maps (road, trail, topographic, etc.)

APPENDIX B

SOURCES OF INFORMATION

The following is a partial list of agencies, associations, and organizations to contact for information on outdoor recreation opportunities in Oregon.

BUREAU OF LAND MANAGEMENT
503-808-6001
blm.gov/contact/oregon-washington

CRATER LAKE NATIONAL PARK
541-594-3000
nps.gov/crla

HELLS CANYON NATIONAL RECREATION AREA (USFS)
541-426-5546 or 541-426-4978
www.fs.usda.gov/wallowa-whitman

THE MAZAMAS (HIKING AND CLIMBING CLUB)
503-227-2345
mazamas.org

OREGON COAST VISITORS ASSOCIATION
541-574-2679 or 888-628-2101
visittheoregoncoast.com

OREGON DEPARTMENT OF FISH AND WILDLIFE
503-947-6000
dfw.state.or.us

OREGON PARKS AND RECREATION DEPARTMENT
503-986-0707 or 800-551-6949
oregonstateparks.org

PORTLAND OREGON FISH AND WILDLIFE OFFICE
503-231-6179
fws.gov/oregonfwo

RESERVATIONS NORTHWEST
800-452-5687
reserveamerica.com

TRAVEL OREGON
800-547-7842
traveloregon.com

U.S. FOREST SERVICE (PACIFIC NORTHWEST REGION)
503-808-2468
www.fs.fed.us/r6

INDEX

Check out this great title from
Menasha Ridge Press!

60 Hikes Within 60 Miles: Portland

By Paul Gerald
ISBN: 978-1-63404-084-6
$18.95, 6th Edition

6x9, paperback
328 pages
full-color photos and maps

The best way to experience Portland is by hiking it! Local author and hiking expert Paul Gerald helps you locate and access the best hikes within a 60-mile radius of the city. These selected trails transport you to scenic overlooks, mountain retreats, and magical forests that renew your spirit and recharge your body. Hike around Mount Hood on the Timberline Trail. See migrating fish in the Salmon River. Enjoy the wildflowers at Tom McCall Preserve in the Columbia River Gorge. Explore the wildlife sanctuary at Oaks Bottom, right in the heart of the city. Stroll behind waterfalls in Silver Falls State Park. Whale watch from high up on Cape Lookout. This book includes expert tips about where to hike and what to expect when you get there, plus key at-a-glance information to quickly and easily learn about each trail. Detailed directions and GPS-based trail maps help guide you along the way.

MENASHA RIDGE PRESS
menasharidge.com

ABOUT THE AUTHOR

Becky Ohlsen is a freelance writer and editor living in Portland, Oregon. Her camping adventures on foot, van, and motorcycle have led her to pitch her tent in many unlikely places, including on a windswept field on a remote Swedish island; inside a stockade in eastern Oregon; behind an abandoned bus outside a Laundromat (also in eastern Oregon); next to a historical school building in Albion, Idaho; tucked beneath a nice family's trailered boat in an overcrowded state park who knows where; atop Rabbit Ears Pass in Colorado; and discreetly off to the side

of the road in any number of places. Her writing has appeared in *The Oregonian, Willamette Week, Lonely Planet* magazine, *Ploughshares,* and *Portland Monthly,* among others. She has written several travel guidebooks for Lonely Planet and is the author of *Walking Portland,* published by Wilderness Press, an imprint of AdventureKEEN.

DEAR CUSTOMERS AND FRIENDS,

SUPPORTING YOUR INTEREST IN OUTDOOR ADVENTURE, travel, and an active lifestyle is central to our operations, from the authors we choose to the locations we detail to the way we design our books. Menasha Ridge Press was incorporated in 1982 by a group of veteran outdoorsmen and professional outfitters. For many years now, we've specialized in creating books that benefit the outdoors enthusiast.

Almost immediately, Menasha Ridge Press earned a reputation for revolutionizing outdoors- and travel-guidebook publishing. For such activities as canoeing, kayaking, hiking, backpacking, and mountain biking, we established new standards of quality that transformed the whole genre, resulting in outdoor-recreation guides of great sophistication and solid content. Menasha Ridge Press continues to be outdoor publishing's greatest innovator.

The folks at Menasha Ridge Press are as at home on a whitewater river or mountain trail as they are editing a manuscript. The books we build for you are the best they can be, because we're responding to your needs. Plus, we use and depend on them ourselves.

We look forward to seeing you on the river or the trail. If you'd like to contact us directly, visit us at menasharidge.com. We thank you for your interest in our books and the natural world around us all.

SAFE TRAVELS,

Bob Sehlinger

**BOB SEHLINGER
PUBLISHER**